SERVICE DESK MANAGER BOOTCAMP

BOOTCAMP

ITIL 4 STANDARDS, KPI & SLA MANAGEMENT

4 BOOKS IN 1

BOOK 1
SERVICE DESK ESSENTIALS: A BEGINNER'S GUIDE TO ITIL 4 STANDARD

BOOK 2
MASTERING KPIS: OPTIMIZING SERVICE DESK PERFORMANCE

BOOK 3
SLA MASTERY: ADVANCED STRATEGIES FOR SERVICE DESK MANAGERS

BOOK 4
BEYOND BASICS: EXPERT INSIGHTS INTO SERVICE DESK MANAGEMENT IN THE DIGITAL AGE

ROB BOTWRIGHT

Published by Rob Botwright
Library of Congress Cataloging-in-Publication Data
ISBN 978-1-83938-746-3
Cover design by Rizzo

Disclaimer

The contents of this book are based on extensive research and the best available historical sources. However, the author and publisher make no claims, promises, or guarantees about the accuracy, completeness, or adequacy of the information contained herein. The information in this book is provided on an "as is" basis, and the author and publisher disclaim any and all liability for any errors, omissions, or inaccuracies in the information or for any actions taken in reliance on such information. The opinions and views expressed in this book are those of the author and do not necessarily reflect the official policy or position of any organization or individual mentioned in this book. Any reference to specific people, places, or events is intended only to provide historical context and is not intended to defame or malign any group, individual, or entity. The information in this book is intended for educational and entertainment purposes only. It is not intended to be a substitute for professional advice or judgment. Readers are encouraged to conduct their own research and to seek professional advice where appropriate. Every effort has been made to obtain necessary permissions and acknowledgments for all images and other copyrighted material used in this book. Any errors or omissions in this regard are unintentional, and the author and publisher will correct them in future editions.

BOOK 1 - SERVICE DESK ESSENTIALS: A BEGINNER'S GUIDE TO ITIL 4 STANDARD

BOOK 2 - MASTERING KPIS: OPTIMIZING SERVICE DESK PERFORMANCE

BOOK 3 - SLA MASTERY: ADVANCED STRATEGIES FOR SERVICE DESK MANAGERS

BOOK 4 - BEYOND BASICS: EXPERT INSIGHTS INTO SERVICE DESK MANAGEMENT IN THE DIGITAL AGE

Introduction

Welcome to the "Service Desk Manager Bootcamp: ITIL 4 Standards, KPI & SLA Management" book bundle. In today's rapidly evolving IT landscape, service desk managers play a crucial role in ensuring efficient and effective delivery of IT services to meet the needs of both internal and external stakeholders. This comprehensive bundle is designed to equip service desk managers with the essential knowledge, skills, and strategies needed to excel in their roles and drive organizational success.

BOOK 1 - Service Desk Essentials: A Beginner's Guide to ITIL 4 Standard: In this foundational book, readers will be introduced to the core principles and practices of ITIL 4, the globally recognized framework for IT service management. From understanding the service lifecycle to implementing best practices for incident, problem, and change management, this book provides a solid foundation for service desk managers to align IT services with business objectives and deliver value to their organizations.

BOOK 2 - Mastering KPIs: Optimizing Service Desk Performance: Effective performance measurement is essential for continuous improvement and success in service desk management. In this book, readers will learn how to identify, define, and track key performance indicators (KPIs) that are aligned with organizational goals. From incident resolution times to customer satisfaction scores, this book provides practical insights and techniques for optimizing service desk performance and enhancing customer satisfaction.

BOOK 3 - SLA Mastery: Advanced Strategies for Service Desk Managers: Service Level Agreements (SLAs) are critical components of service delivery, defining the expectations and commitments between service providers and customers. In this advanced book, readers will explore strategies for negotiating, implementing, and managing SLAs to ensure compliance and alignment with business objectives. From defining service metrics to resolving SLA breaches, this book provides expert guidance and strategies for SLA mastery.

BOOK 4 - Beyond Basics: Expert Insights into Service Desk Management in the Digital Age: As technology continues to evolve, service desk managers must adapt to new challenges and opportunities in the digital age. In this insightful book, readers will gain expert insights and practical strategies for leveraging emerging technologies, managing remote teams, and delivering exceptional customer experiences in today's digital landscape. From chatbots to predictive analytics, this book explores innovative approaches and best practices for service desk management in the digital age.

Together, these four books form a comprehensive guidebook for service desk managers looking to excel in their roles and drive organizational success through ITIL 4 standards, KPI optimization, SLA mastery, and expert insights into service desk management in the digital age. Whether you're a beginner looking to build a strong foundation or an experienced manager seeking advanced strategies, this book bundle has something for everyone on their journey to service desk excellence.

BOOK 1
SERVICE DESK ESSENTIALS
A BEGINNER'S GUIDE TO ITIL 4 STANDARD

ROB BOTWRIGHT

Chapter 1: Introduction to IT Service Management

Core Concepts in IT Service Management (ITSM) form the foundational framework upon which the entire discipline operates. At its essence, ITSM revolves around delivering value to customers through the effective and efficient management of IT services. Central to this concept is the notion of service, which encapsulates the provision of utility and warranty to meet customer needs and expectations. In the realm of ITSM, services are not merely products or technology components but rather the means through which value is co-created with customers. This shift in perspective underscores the importance of aligning IT activities and resources with business objectives and customer requirements.

One of the fundamental principles of ITSM is the adoption of a process-oriented approach to service delivery and management. Processes serve as the means through which activities are coordinated and executed to achieve specific objectives. These processes are designed to be systematic, repeatable, and measurable, facilitating consistency and predictability in service outcomes. Key processes in ITSM include incident management, problem management, change management, and service level management, each playing a crucial role in ensuring the reliability and quality of IT services.

Incident management focuses on restoring normal service operation as quickly as possible following an unplanned disruption or degradation in service quality. Through the timely identification, categorization, prioritization, and resolution of incidents, organizations can minimize the impact on business operations and customer satisfaction. Tools such as service desk software and ticketing systems are commonly utilized to facilitate the efficient handling of incidents, enabling IT teams to track and manage incidents from inception to resolution.

Similarly, problem management seeks to address the root causes of recurring incidents and prevent future occurrences. By conducting thorough investigations, root cause analyses, and implementing corrective actions, organizations can proactively identify and resolve underlying issues within the IT infrastructure. This proactive approach not only reduces the frequency and impact of incidents but also contributes to overall service improvement and stability.

Change management is another critical process in ITSM that focuses on managing the introduction of changes to IT services in a controlled and coordinated manner. Recognizing that changes carry inherent risks to service stability and performance, change management aims to minimize disruptions while maximizing the benefits of change. This involves assessing the impact and risks of proposed changes, obtaining appropriate approvals, and implementing changes through standardized procedures and protocols. Configuration management databases (CMDBs) and change management tools play a vital role in facilitating change control and documentation.

Service level management (SLM) is the process responsible for defining, negotiating, and managing service level agreements (SLAs) with customers and stakeholders. SLAs establish clear expectations regarding the quality, availability, and performance of IT services, serving as the basis for measuring and reporting service performance. Through ongoing monitoring, measurement, and review, SLM ensures that services align with business objectives and meet agreed-upon service levels. This proactive approach enables organizations to identify areas for improvement and drive continuous service optimization.

Central to the success of ITSM is the adoption of a customer-centric mindset, wherein the needs and experiences of customers are prioritized throughout the service lifecycle. This customer focus extends beyond the delivery of IT services to encompass the entire user experience, from initial engagement to ongoing support and feedback. By understanding and anticipating customer requirements, organizations can tailor services to meet specific needs, enhance satisfaction, and foster long-term relationships.

In addition to process orientation and customer focus, ITSM emphasizes the importance of continual improvement as a core guiding principle. Continual service improvement (CSI) encourages organizations to regularly evaluate performance, identify opportunities for enhancement, and implement changes to drive ongoing value creation. Through the systematic application of the Plan-Do-Check-Act (PDCA) cycle, organizations can iteratively improve processes, services, and overall ITSM capabilities.

Technological advancements and industry trends continue to shape the landscape of ITSM, introducing new opportunities and challenges for organizations. The proliferation of digital technologies, such as cloud computing, artificial intelligence, and automation, has revolutionized the way IT services are delivered and consumed. Organizations must adapt to these changes by embracing innovation, leveraging emerging technologies, and evolving their ITSM practices to remain competitive in today's dynamic business environment.

In summary, core concepts in ITSM provide the foundational framework for effective service delivery and management in the digital age. By embracing process orientation, customer focus, continual improvement, and adapting to technological advancements, organizations can enhance service quality, drive operational excellence, and achieve strategic business objectives.

Importance of IT Service Management cannot be overstated in today's digital landscape where organizations rely heavily on technology to drive business operations, enhance productivity, and deliver value to customers. IT Service Management (ITSM) encompasses a set of practices, policies, and procedures designed to align IT services with the needs of the business and ensure the delivery of high-quality services. At its core, ITSM is about establishing a structured approach to managing IT services throughout their lifecycle, from design and development to operation and improvement.

One of the primary reasons for the importance of ITSM is its role in enabling organizations to effectively harness the power of technology to achieve their strategic objectives. In an increasingly competitive marketplace, businesses must leverage IT resources efficiently and strategically to gain a competitive edge. ITSM provides the framework and discipline necessary to optimize the use of IT assets, streamline processes, and deliver services that meet or exceed customer expectations. By aligning IT with business goals, organizations can drive innovation, improve operational efficiency, and enhance overall business performance.

Central to the importance of ITSM is its focus on delivering value to customers. In today's service-oriented economy, customer satisfaction and loyalty are paramount to business success. ITSM emphasizes the importance of understanding customer needs and expectations and delivering services that provide tangible benefits and outcomes. Through the adoption of customer-centric practices such as service level agreements (SLAs), service catalogs, and customer feedback mechanisms, organizations can ensure that IT services are aligned with business requirements and deliver value that is measurable and demonstrable.

Another key aspect of the importance of ITSM is its role in ensuring the reliability and availability of IT services. In today's interconnected and digital world, downtime and disruptions can have far-reaching consequences for businesses, ranging from financial losses to damage to reputation. ITSM practices such as incident management, problem management, and change management are essential for minimizing the impact of service outages and restoring normal operations quickly and efficiently. By implementing robust processes and controls, organizations can enhance the resilience of their IT infrastructure and minimize the risk of service disruptions.

Moreover, the importance of ITSM extends beyond day-to-day operations to encompass strategic planning and decision-making. ITSM provides organizations with the tools and insights they need to make informed decisions about their IT investments, resources, and priorities. Through techniques such as service portfolio management, demand management, and financial management, organizations can allocate resources effectively, prioritize investments, and optimize the value delivered by IT services. This strategic approach enables organizations to align IT with business objectives, drive innovation, and capitalize on emerging opportunities in the marketplace.

Furthermore, ITSM plays a crucial role in ensuring regulatory compliance and mitigating risks. In today's complex regulatory environment, organizations face a myriad of compliance requirements related to data privacy, security, and governance. ITSM provides the framework and controls necessary to ensure that IT services comply with relevant regulations and standards. By implementing policies and procedures for risk management, security management, and compliance auditing, organizations can mitigate risks, protect sensitive data, and maintain the trust and confidence of stakeholders.

Additionally, the importance of ITSM is underscored by its contribution to organizational agility and adaptability. In today's fast-paced and dynamic business environment, organizations must be able to respond quickly to changing market conditions, customer demands, and technological advancements. ITSM practices such as service design, service transition, and continual service improvement enable organizations to adapt and evolve their IT services in response to changing business needs. By fostering a culture of innovation, learning, and continuous improvement, organizations can stay ahead of the curve and remain competitive in the digital age.

In summary, the importance of IT Service Management cannot be overstated in today's digital era. By providing a structured approach to managing IT services, aligning IT with business objectives, delivering value to customers, ensuring reliability and availability, facilitating strategic decision-making, ensuring regulatory compliance, and fostering organizational agility, ITSM enables organizations to maximize the value of their IT investments, drive business success, and thrive in an increasingly competitive marketplace.

Chapter 2: Understanding the ITIL Framework

History and Evolution of ITIL is a fascinating journey that traces the development of a framework that has become synonymous with best practices in IT Service Management (ITSM). ITIL, which stands for Information Technology Infrastructure Library, originated in the late 1980s in the United Kingdom as a response to the growing need for standardized practices in IT service delivery. Developed by the Central Computer and Telecommunications Agency (CCTA), a government agency in the UK, ITIL was initially intended as a set of recommendations for improving the efficiency and effectiveness of IT operations within government organizations.

The first version of ITIL, known as ITIL v1, was published in the early 1990s and consisted of a series of books that outlined best practices for various aspects of IT service management, such as service support and service delivery. ITIL v1 was based on a process-oriented approach to ITSM and introduced concepts such as incident management, problem management, change management, and configuration management. While ITIL v1 laid the foundation for modern ITSM practices, it was not widely adopted outside of government organizations in the UK.

In the early 2000s, the UK government recognized the potential value of ITIL beyond its borders and decided to make the framework available to the public. In 2001, the CCTA was disbanded, and responsibility for ITIL was transferred to the Office of Government Commerce (OGC). The OGC worked with various stakeholders, including IT practitioners, consultants, and training providers, to revise and update ITIL to make it more accessible and applicable to a broader audience.

The result of this collaborative effort was the release of ITIL v2 in 2001, which represented a significant evolution of the framework. ITIL v2 consisted of a set of eight core publications, known as the ITIL Service Management Practices, covering topics such as service support, service delivery, security management, and application management. ITIL v2 also introduced the concept of the IT service lifecycle, which emphasized the importance of viewing IT services from a holistic perspective, from initial concept to retirement.

One of the key strengths of ITIL v2 was its flexibility and scalability, which made it suitable for organizations of all sizes and industries. ITIL v2 provided organizations with a common language and set of processes for managing IT services, enabling them to improve service quality, reduce costs, and increase customer satisfaction. As a result, ITIL v2 gained widespread adoption around the world and became the de facto standard for ITSM in many organizations.

However, ITIL v2 was not without its limitations. Critics argued that the framework was overly complex and prescriptive, making it difficult to implement and customize to meet the unique needs of different organizations. In response to these concerns, the OGC embarked on a project to update and improve ITIL, leading to the development of ITIL v3.

Released in 2007, ITIL v3 represented a significant departure from its predecessor, introducing a more holistic and integrated approach to ITSM. ITIL v3 expanded upon the concept of the IT service lifecycle introduced in ITIL v2, reorganizing the framework into five core publications, known as the ITIL Service Lifecycle Suite. These publications covered the entire lifecycle of IT services, from strategy to design, transition, operation, and continual improvement.

One of the key innovations of ITIL v3 was the introduction of the Service Strategy publication, which emphasized the importance of aligning IT services with business objectives and customer needs. ITIL v3 also introduced new processes and concepts, such as service portfolio management, demand management, and business relationship management, to help organizations deliver more value to their customers.

In 2011, ITIL underwent another major revision with the release of ITIL 2011. ITIL 2011 represented a minor update to ITIL v3, incorporating feedback from practitioners and clarifying certain concepts and processes. While the core principles and practices of ITIL remained unchanged, ITIL 2011 provided organizations with updated guidance and best practices to address emerging trends and challenges in ITSM.

In recent years, ITIL has continued to evolve in response to changes in technology, business, and industry trends. In 2019, Axelos, the organization responsible for managing ITIL, announced the release of ITIL 4, the latest iteration of the framework. ITIL 4 builds upon the core principles of its predecessors while incorporating new concepts such as the Service Value System (SVS), the Four Dimensions of Service Management, and the Service Value Chain.

One of the key objectives of ITIL 4 is to modernize the framework and make it more relevant and adaptable to the digital age. ITIL 4 emphasizes the importance of agility, flexibility, and collaboration in ITSM, reflecting the shift towards DevOps, Agile, and Lean methodologies. By embracing these principles, organizations can better respond to changing customer needs, accelerate service delivery, and drive innovation in IT service management.

In summary, the history and evolution of ITIL reflect the ongoing quest for excellence in IT service management. From its humble beginnings as a government initiative in the UK to its global adoption as the standard framework for ITSM, ITIL has undergone numerous transformations to remain relevant and effective in a rapidly changing world. As organizations continue to navigate the complexities of the digital age, ITIL will continue to evolve to meet the evolving needs and challenges of the IT industry.

Key Components of the ITIL Framework encompass a comprehensive set of concepts, principles, and practices that are essential for effective IT Service Management (ITSM). ITIL, which stands for Information Technology Infrastructure Library, is a globally recognized framework that provides guidance on best practices for managing IT services and aligning them with the needs of the business. At the heart of the ITIL framework are several key components that form the building blocks for successful ITSM implementation and operation.

One of the central components of the ITIL framework is the Service Lifecycle, which provides a structured approach to managing IT services from inception to retirement. The Service Lifecycle consists of five stages: Service Strategy, Service Design, Service Transition, Service Operation, and Continual Service Improvement. Each stage represents a distinct phase in the lifecycle of an IT service and is characterized by specific activities, processes, and deliverables.

The first stage of the Service Lifecycle is Service Strategy, which focuses on defining the strategic objectives and priorities of IT services in alignment with the overall business strategy. Service Strategy involves assessing market demand, identifying opportunities for service innovation, and developing a strategic plan for delivering value to customers. Key processes in Service Strategy include Service Portfolio Management, Demand Management, and Financial Management for IT Services.

Once the strategic direction for IT services has been established, the next stage is Service Design, which involves designing and developing IT services that meet the needs and expectations of customers and stakeholders. Service Design encompasses activities such as designing service architectures, specifying service level requirements, and defining service transition plans. Key processes in Service Design include

Service Catalog Management, Service Level Management, and Capacity Management.

The third stage of the Service Lifecycle is Service Transition, which focuses on transitioning new or modified IT services into the live environment while minimizing disruptions to business operations. Service Transition involves activities such as testing, training, and deploying new services, as well as managing changes to existing services. Key processes in Service Transition include Change Management, Release and Deployment Management, and Knowledge Management.

Once IT services are operational, the focus shifts to Service Operation, which is responsible for delivering and supporting IT services on a day-to-day basis. Service Operation involves activities such as incident management, problem management, and request fulfillment, as well as monitoring service performance and ensuring service availability and reliability. Key processes in Service Operation include Incident Management, Problem Management, and Event Management.

The final stage of the Service Lifecycle is Continual Service Improvement (CSI), which focuses on identifying opportunities for enhancing the quality and efficiency of IT services through ongoing measurement, analysis, and improvement. CSI involves activities such as reviewing service performance, identifying areas for improvement, and implementing corrective actions. Key processes in Continual Service Improvement include

Service Measurement and Reporting, Service Review Meetings, and Service Improvement Plans.

In addition to the Service Lifecycle, the ITIL framework includes several other key components that are essential for effective ITSM. One such component is the ITIL Process Model, which provides a structured approach to managing IT services through a set of interrelated processes. The ITIL Process Model defines a series of processes that cover the entire lifecycle of an IT service, from strategy to operation to improvement.

Another key component of the ITIL framework is the ITIL Functions, which represent specialized teams or groups within an organization that are responsible for performing specific activities or tasks related to IT service management. Examples of ITIL Functions include the Service Desk, which provides a single point of contact for users to request assistance and report incidents, and the Technical Management Function, which is responsible for managing the technical infrastructure that supports IT services.

Furthermore, the ITIL framework includes a set of Key Principles that provide guiding principles for effective IT service management. These principles, which include focusing on value, designing for experience, and ensuring simplicity and practicality, serve as the foundation for ITIL's best practices and help organizations achieve their ITSM objectives.

Overall, the key components of the ITIL framework provide organizations with a comprehensive and structured approach to managing IT services and delivering value to customers. By understanding and implementing these components effectively, organizations can improve service quality, reduce costs, and enhance customer satisfaction, ultimately driving business success.

Chapter 3: Overview of ITIL 4 Standard

Key Changes and Updates in ITIL 4 reflect a significant evolution of the framework to meet the evolving needs and challenges of the digital age. ITIL, which stands for Information Technology Infrastructure Library, has undergone several revisions since its inception in the late 1980s, with each iteration reflecting changes in technology, business practices, and industry trends. ITIL 4, the latest iteration of the framework, represents a major overhaul that introduces new concepts, principles, and practices to help organizations navigate the complexities of modern IT service management.

One of the key changes in ITIL 4 is the introduction of the Service Value System (SVS), which replaces the Service Lifecycle approach used in previous versions of ITIL. The SVS is a holistic approach to managing IT services that emphasizes the creation of value for customers and stakeholders. At the core of the SVS is the Service Value Chain, which represents a series of interconnected activities that organizations can use to create value for their customers. The Service Value Chain consists of six key activities: Plan, Improve, Engage, Design and Transition, Obtain/Build, and Deliver and Support.

Another significant change in ITIL 4 is the adoption of a more flexible and adaptable approach to IT service management. Unlike previous versions of ITIL, which were prescriptive and process-oriented, ITIL 4 emphasizes the importance of agility, collaboration, and continuous improvement. This shift reflects the growing recognition that traditional ITSM practices are no longer sufficient to meet the rapidly changing demands of the digital economy. Instead, organizations must be able to respond quickly to changing market conditions, customer needs, and technological advancements.

To facilitate this shift towards agility and flexibility, ITIL 4 introduces several new concepts and practices. One such concept is the Four Dimensions of Service Management, which represent the key factors that organizations must consider when designing and delivering IT services. The Four Dimensions include Organizations and People, Information and Technology, Partners and Suppliers, and Value Streams and Processes. By considering these dimensions holistically, organizations can ensure that their IT services are aligned with business objectives, customer needs, and market trends.

Additionally, ITIL 4 introduces the concept of the ITIL Guiding Principles, which provide organizations with a set of guiding principles for effective IT service management. These principles, which include focusing on value, collaborating and promoting visibility, and starting where you are, serve as the foundation for ITIL 4's best practices and help organizations navigate complex and dynamic environments. By adhering to these principles, organizations can make informed decisions, drive continuous improvement, and achieve better outcomes for their customers and stakeholders.

In addition to these conceptual changes, ITIL 4 also introduces several new practices and techniques to help organizations improve their IT service management capabilities. One such practice is the Service Value Stream, which represents the end-to-end process for delivering a specific service to customers. By mapping out the Service Value Stream, organizations can identify opportunities for streamlining processes, eliminating waste, and improving service delivery.

Another new practice in ITIL 4 is the Service Configuration Management practice, which focuses on maintaining accurate and up-to-date information about the configuration of IT services and components. By establishing a centralized repository of configuration data, organizations can improve visibility into their IT infrastructure, reduce the risk of service disruptions, and enhance the effectiveness of change management processes.

Furthermore, ITIL 4 introduces the concept of Value Streams, which represent the series of steps required to deliver value to customers through the provision of products and services. By identifying and optimizing Value Streams, organizations can streamline processes, eliminate waste, and improve the overall efficiency and effectiveness of their IT service delivery.

Overall, the key changes and updates in ITIL 4 represent a significant step forward in the evolution of the framework. By embracing concepts such as the Service Value System, Four Dimensions of Service Management, ITIL Guiding Principles, and new practices and techniques, organizations can enhance their IT service management capabilities and better meet the needs and expectations of their customers and stakeholders in the digital age.

Principles and Practices in ITIL 4 Standard form the cornerstone of modern IT Service Management (ITSM), providing organizations with a comprehensive framework for delivering value to customers and stakeholders. ITIL, which stands for Information Technology Infrastructure Library, has evolved over several decades to keep pace with changes in technology, business practices, and industry trends. ITIL 4, the latest iteration of the framework, introduces a set of guiding principles and practices that reflect the dynamic and complex nature of the digital economy.

At the heart of ITIL 4 are the Seven Guiding Principles, which provide organizations with a set of core beliefs and values that should guide their decision-making and actions in ITSM. These principles, which include focusing on value, starting where you are, and keeping it simple and practical, serve as the foundation for ITIL 4's best practices and help organizations navigate the complexities of modern IT service delivery.

One of the key principles in ITIL 4 is the focus on value, which emphasizes the importance of delivering value to customers and stakeholders through the provision of products and services. To achieve this principle, organizations must understand the needs and expectations of their customers, identify opportunities for value creation, and continuously improve their IT services to meet changing demands.

Another key principle in ITIL 4 is the focus on collaboration and teamwork, which recognizes that successful IT service delivery requires cooperation and coordination across different teams and departments within an organization. By fostering a culture of collaboration and promoting cross-functional teamwork, organizations can break down silos, improve communication, and enhance overall service delivery.

Furthermore, ITIL 4 emphasizes the importance of taking a holistic and integrated approach to IT service management, which involves considering the entire service lifecycle, from strategy to operation to improvement. This principle encourages organizations to view IT services as interconnected and interdependent, with each stage of the service lifecycle contributing to the overall value delivered to customers and stakeholders.

Moreover, ITIL 4 promotes the adoption of a flexible and adaptive mindset, which recognizes that change is inevitable in the dynamic and rapidly evolving digital economy. By embracing change and being willing to adapt to new technologies, methodologies, and business practices, organizations can stay ahead of the curve and remain competitive in today's marketplace.

In addition to the guiding principles, ITIL 4 introduces several new practices and techniques to help organizations improve their IT service management capabilities. One such practice is the Service Value System (SVS), which provides organizations with a holistic approach to managing IT services and delivering value to customers. The SVS consists of several components, including the Service Value Chain, Service Value Streams, and the Four Dimensions of Service Management, which together form the foundation for effective IT service delivery.

Another new practice in ITIL 4 is the concept of the Service Value Chain, which represents a series of interconnected activities that organizations can use to create value for their customers. The Service Value Chain consists of six key activities: Plan, Improve, Engage, Design and Transition, Obtain/Build, and Deliver and Support. By understanding and optimizing these activities, organizations can improve their ability to deliver value to customers and stakeholders.

Furthermore, ITIL 4 introduces the concept of Value Streams, which represent the series of steps required to deliver value to customers through the provision of products and services. By identifying and optimizing Value Streams, organizations can streamline processes, eliminate waste, and improve the overall efficiency and effectiveness of their IT service delivery.

Overall, the principles and practices in ITIL 4 Standard provide organizations with a comprehensive and flexible framework for delivering value to customers and stakeholders in the digital age. By embracing the guiding principles, adopting new practices and techniques, and taking a holistic and integrated approach to IT service management, organizations can improve service quality, reduce costs, and enhance customer satisfaction, ultimately driving business success.

Chapter 4: Service Desk Fundamentals

Role and Responsibilities of a Service Desk are paramount in the realm of IT Service Management (ITSM), serving as the frontline support for end-users and the central point of contact between customers and IT service providers. The Service Desk plays a critical role in ensuring the delivery of high-quality IT services and maintaining customer satisfaction. At its core, the Service Desk is responsible for handling incidents, service requests, and inquiries from users, resolving issues in a timely and efficient manner to minimize disruption to business operations and maximize productivity.

One of the primary responsibilities of the Service Desk is to serve as the single point of contact for users seeking assistance with IT-related issues. Users can reach out to the Service Desk through various channels, including phone calls, emails, web portals, and self-service options. Upon receiving a request for assistance, Service Desk agents are responsible for logging the incident or service request into the IT service management system and assigning it an appropriate priority based on its impact and urgency.

To effectively manage incidents and service requests, Service Desk agents must possess strong communication and interpersonal skills, as well as technical expertise in troubleshooting and problem-solving. Service Desk agents are often the first point of contact for users experiencing technical issues, and as such, they must be able to listen attentively to users' concerns, ask probing questions to gather relevant information, and provide clear and concise instructions for resolving the issue.

In addition to handling incidents and service requests, the Service Desk is also responsible for providing timely updates and status reports to users regarding the progress of their requests. Service Desk agents must keep users informed of any developments or changes to their requests, including estimated resolution times and any workarounds or temporary solutions that may be available. Effective communication is key to maintaining customer satisfaction and confidence in the IT service provider.

Furthermore, the Service Desk is responsible for maintaining accurate and up-to-date records of all incidents and service requests logged with the IT service management system. This includes documenting relevant details such as the nature of the issue, steps taken to resolve it, and any follow-up actions required. By maintaining comprehensive records, the Service Desk can track trends, identify recurring issues, and identify opportunities for process improvement.

Moreover, the Service Desk plays a vital role in facilitating the resolution of incidents and service requests by coordinating with other teams and support groups within the IT organization. Service Desk agents may escalate incidents to higher-level support groups or subject matter experts if they are unable to resolve them independently. Similarly, they may collaborate with other teams, such as the network team, server team, or application support team, to troubleshoot complex issues that require specialized expertise.

To effectively manage and prioritize incidents and service requests, many organizations rely on IT service management tools and software, such as ServiceNow, Jira Service Desk, or Zendesk. These tools provide Service Desk agents with a centralized platform for logging, tracking, and managing incidents and service requests, as well as generating reports and analytics to monitor performance and identify areas for improvement.

In addition to handling reactive support activities, the Service Desk also plays a proactive role in preventing incidents and minimizing service disruptions through knowledge management and user education. Service Desk agents are responsible for documenting known errors and solutions in a knowledge base, which can be accessed by users for self-service troubleshooting. They may also conduct training sessions or create user guides and documentation to help users avoid common issues and improve their IT literacy.

Furthermore, the Service Desk is often responsible for monitoring the performance and availability of IT services and infrastructure, proactively identifying potential issues or bottlenecks before they escalate into major incidents. Service Desk agents may use monitoring tools such as Nagios, SolarWinds, or Zabbix to monitor key performance indicators (KPIs) and alert thresholds, enabling them to take corrective action quickly to prevent service disruptions.

Overall, the role and responsibilities of a Service Desk are multifaceted and critical to the success of IT service delivery. By serving as the central point of contact for users, providing timely and effective support, maintaining accurate records, coordinating with other support groups, and proactively preventing incidents, the Service Desk plays a crucial role in ensuring the reliability, availability, and performance of IT services and infrastructure.

Service Desk Structure and Models are crucial components of IT Service Management (ITSM), providing organizations with a framework for delivering efficient and effective support to end-users and customers. The structure of a Service Desk typically encompasses various elements, including organizational hierarchy, staffing levels, processes, and tools, all of which are designed to ensure the smooth operation of IT services and the timely resolution of incidents and service requests.

One common model for structuring a Service Desk is the Tiered Support Model, which organizes support activities into multiple tiers or levels based on the complexity of the issues and the expertise required to resolve them. In this model, Tier 1 support handles basic inquiries and common issues, such as password resets and software installations, while Tier 2 support deals with more complex technical issues that cannot be resolved at the Tier 1 level. Tier 3 support, also known as escalation support, consists of specialized teams or subject matter experts who handle highly complex or specialized issues that require advanced technical knowledge or specialized skills.

To implement the Tiered Support Model effectively, organizations must establish clear escalation procedures and guidelines for determining when an issue should be escalated to a higher tier. This may involve defining criteria such as the severity of the issue, the impact on business operations, and the availability of resources and expertise at each tier. By establishing clear escalation pathways, organizations can ensure that incidents are resolved in a timely and efficient manner, while also providing a consistent and seamless support experience for end-users.

Another common model for structuring a Service Desk is the Follow the Sun Model, which leverages global resources and time zone differences to provide around-the-clock support to users in different regions. In this model, organizations establish multiple Service Desk locations in different geographic regions, each staffed with support agents who work during regular business hours in their respective time zones. As the day progresses and one Service Desk location closes, support activities are seamlessly transitioned to the next location, ensuring uninterrupted support coverage for users worldwide.

To implement the Follow the Sun Model effectively, organizations must establish robust communication and collaboration processes between Service Desk locations to facilitate the seamless transfer of incidents and service requests. This may involve implementing shared ticketing systems, communication channels, and knowledge management platforms to ensure that support agents have access to the information and resources they need to resolve issues effectively. By leveraging global resources and time zone differences, organizations can improve service availability, reduce response times, and enhance customer satisfaction.

In addition to the Tiered Support Model and the Follow the Sun Model, organizations may also choose to adopt a Hybrid Service Desk Model, which combines elements of both centralized and decentralized support structures. In this model, organizations maintain a central Service Desk function to handle common inquiries and routine support activities, while also establishing regional or departmental support teams to provide specialized support for specific business units or geographic regions.

To implement a Hybrid Service Desk Model effectively, organizations must strike a balance between centralized control and decentralized autonomy, ensuring that support activities are coordinated and aligned with overall business objectives while also allowing for flexibility and responsiveness to local needs and preferences. This may involve establishing clear roles and responsibilities for each support team, implementing standardized processes and procedures, and providing ongoing training and support to ensure consistency and quality of service across all support channels.

Regardless of the specific model adopted, successful Service Desk structure and models require careful planning, implementation, and ongoing management to ensure that support activities are aligned with business goals, customer needs, and industry best practices. By establishing clear roles and responsibilities, implementing standardized processes and procedures, leveraging appropriate tools and technologies, and providing ongoing training and support to staff, organizations can create a Service Desk structure that delivers efficient and effective support to end-users and customers, ultimately driving business success.

Chapter 5: Incident Management Basics

Incident Identification and Classification are fundamental processes in IT Service Management (ITSM), essential for maintaining the stability and reliability of IT services and minimizing disruption to business operations. Incident identification involves recognizing and acknowledging issues or abnormalities within the IT environment that have the potential to impact service availability or performance, while incident classification involves categorizing incidents based on their nature, severity, and impact on business operations.

To effectively identify incidents, organizations rely on a variety of monitoring tools and technologies that provide visibility into the performance and health of IT services and infrastructure. These tools may include network monitoring systems, server monitoring tools, application performance monitoring (APM) solutions, and security information and event management (SIEM) platforms, among others. By continuously monitoring key performance indicators (KPIs), such as system uptime, response times, and error rates, organizations can quickly detect anomalies or deviations from normal operating conditions that may indicate the presence of an incident.

Once an incident has been identified, the next step is to classify it based on its nature, severity, and impact on business operations. Incident classification typically involves assigning a priority and severity level to the incident, as well as categorizing it into predefined incident categories or types. This allows organizations to prioritize their response efforts and allocate resources accordingly, ensuring that critical incidents receive prompt attention and resolution.

To classify incidents effectively, organizations may use predefined incident classification schemes or taxonomies that provide a standardized framework for categorizing and prioritizing incidents. These classification schemes typically include categories such as hardware failures, software errors, user errors, security incidents, and service requests, each with its own set of criteria for determining priority and severity.

One commonly used incident classification scheme is the ITIL Incident Priority Matrix, which categorizes incidents based on their impact and urgency. In this matrix, incidents are classified into four priority levels: Priority 1 (Critical), Priority 2 (High), Priority 3 (Medium), and Priority 4 (Low). The priority level of an incident is determined by assessing its impact on business operations and the urgency of the issue, with critical incidents being those that have the highest impact and require immediate attention.

To classify incidents using the ITIL Incident Priority Matrix, organizations typically use a combination of quantitative and qualitative criteria to assess the impact and urgency of the incident. Quantitative criteria may include metrics such as the number of users affected, the extent of service downtime, and the financial impact on the business, while qualitative criteria may include factors such as the criticality of the affected service or the potential for reputational damage.

Once the impact and urgency of the incident have been assessed, organizations can assign a priority level based on predefined thresholds and criteria. For example, incidents that have a high impact on critical business functions and require immediate resolution may be classified as Priority 1 (Critical), while incidents that have a lower impact and can be addressed within a reasonable timeframe may be classified as Priority 2 (High) or Priority 3 (Medium).

In addition to assigning a priority level, incidents may also be classified based on their severity, which reflects the extent of the impact on business operations and the urgency of the issue. Severity levels may include categories such as Sev-1 (Critical), Sev-2 (High), Sev-3 (Medium), and Sev-4 (Low), each with its own set of criteria for determining severity.

Once incidents have been identified and classified, organizations can initiate the incident management process to investigate, diagnose, and resolve the issue in a timely and effective manner. This may involve coordinating with various support teams and stakeholders, implementing workarounds or temporary fixes to restore service availability, and implementing permanent solutions to prevent recurrence of the incident.

Overall, incident identification and classification are critical processes in ITSM that enable organizations to quickly detect and respond to issues within the IT environment, minimize disruption to business operations, and maintain high levels of service availability and performance. By leveraging monitoring tools, predefined classification schemes, and incident management processes, organizations can streamline incident handling processes, improve response times, and enhance customer satisfaction.

Incident Prioritization and Escalation are critical components of the incident management process in IT Service Management (ITSM), essential for ensuring that resources are allocated effectively and that critical issues are addressed in a timely manner. Incident prioritization involves categorizing incidents based on their impact, urgency, and severity, while incident escalation involves escalating incidents to higher levels of support or management when necessary to ensure timely resolution.

To prioritize incidents effectively, organizations typically use predefined prioritization criteria or matrices that classify incidents based on their impact on business operations and the urgency of the issue. One commonly used prioritization matrix is the ITIL Incident Priority Matrix, which categorizes incidents into four priority levels: Priority 1 (Critical), Priority 2 (High), Priority 3 (Medium), and Priority 4 (Low). This matrix takes into account factors such as the number of users affected, the extent of service downtime, and the financial impact on the business to determine the priority level of each incident.

To assign priority levels to incidents, organizations may use a combination of quantitative and qualitative criteria, such as severity, impact, and urgency. For example, incidents that have a high impact on critical business functions and require immediate resolution may be classified as Priority 1 (Critical), while incidents that have a lower impact and can be addressed within a reasonable timeframe may be classified as Priority 2 (High) or Priority 3 (Medium).

Once incidents have been prioritized, the next step is to determine the appropriate escalation path based on the priority level and severity of the incident. Incident escalation involves transferring ownership of the incident to higher levels of support or management when the current support team is unable to resolve the issue within the defined timeframe or when additional resources or expertise are required.

To escalate incidents effectively, organizations must establish clear escalation procedures and guidelines that define when and how incidents should be escalated. This may involve defining escalation thresholds based on the priority level and severity of the incident, as well as establishing escalation contacts and communication channels for each support team or level of escalation.

For example, organizations may define escalation thresholds that specify when incidents should be escalated from Tier 1 support to Tier 2 support, or from Tier 2 support to Tier 3 support. They may also designate specific individuals or roles as escalation contacts who are responsible for overseeing the escalation process and ensuring that incidents are escalated and resolved in a timely manner.

To initiate an escalation, support agents typically use ITSM tools and systems to update the incident record and notify the appropriate escalation contact or team. For example, in a ticketing system such as ServiceNow or Jira Service Desk, support agents may use the "escalate" command or option to transfer ownership of the incident to a higher level of support or management. This triggers an automatic notification to the designated escalation contact or team, who then assumes responsibility for resolving the incident.

In addition to manual escalation, organizations may also use automated escalation rules and workflows to streamline the escalation process and ensure that incidents are escalated promptly when necessary. For example, organizations may define escalation rules that automatically escalate incidents based on predefined criteria, such as the elapsed time since the incident was logged or the number of failed attempts to resolve the issue.

By establishing clear prioritization criteria and escalation procedures, organizations can ensure that critical incidents receive prompt attention and resolution, while also providing a consistent and transparent escalation process for support teams and stakeholders. This helps to minimize downtime, reduce the impact on business operations, and enhance customer satisfaction.

Chapter 6: Problem Management Essentials

Root Cause Analysis (RCA) Techniques are essential tools in the arsenal of IT Service Management (ITSM) professionals, enabling them to identify the underlying causes of incidents, problems, and failures within the IT environment and implement effective solutions to prevent recurrence. RCA is a systematic process that involves investigating and analyzing the events leading up to an incident or problem, identifying contributing factors and root causes, and implementing corrective actions to address underlying issues.

One common technique used in RCA is the "5 Whys" method, which involves asking a series of "why" questions to uncover deeper layers of causality behind an incident or problem. This technique is based on the premise that by repeatedly asking "why" a problem occurred, one can trace the root cause back to its underlying source. For example, if an incident occurred due to a server outage, the first "why" question might be "Why did the server go down?" followed by subsequent "why" questions to uncover factors such as inadequate maintenance, insufficient capacity planning, or hardware failures.

To perform a "5 Whys" analysis, ITSM professionals can use a simple text editor or document software to document each "why" question and its corresponding answer. Alternatively, they may use specialized RCA software or tools that are designed to facilitate the RCA process and provide features such as branching logic, automated workflows, and collaboration capabilities. For example, teams may use tools like Fishbone Diagrams, Ishikawa Diagrams, or Mind Maps to visually map out the causal relationships between different factors and identify potential root causes.

Another popular RCA technique is the Fishbone Diagram, also known as the Ishikawa Diagram or Cause-and-Effect Diagram, which provides a structured approach to identifying and categorizing potential root causes of an issue. The Fishbone Diagram consists of a central "spine" representing the problem or effect, with branches extending outward to represent different categories of potential causes, such as people, processes, equipment, environment, and management. By systematically brainstorming potential causes within each category and analyzing their relationships, teams can uncover root causes and contributing factors that may have otherwise been overlooked.

To create a Fishbone Diagram, teams can use specialized software or drawing tools that provide templates and pre-defined shapes for constructing the diagram. Alternatively, they may use a whiteboard or flip chart to sketch out the diagram manually during a brainstorming session or RCA workshop. Once the diagram has been created, teams can analyze the relationships between different causes and prioritize potential root causes for further investigation and analysis.

Additionally, organizations may use statistical analysis techniques such as Pareto Analysis or Trend Analysis to identify patterns and trends in incident data and prioritize potential root causes based on their frequency or impact. Pareto Analysis, also known as the 80/20 rule, involves identifying the most significant contributors to a problem or issue and focusing efforts on addressing those factors first. Trend Analysis involves analyzing historical incident data over time to identify recurring patterns or trends that may indicate underlying systemic issues.

To perform statistical analysis, teams may use spreadsheet software such as Microsoft Excel or specialized data analysis tools that provide built-in functions and capabilities for calculating frequencies, percentages, and trends. By analyzing incident data and identifying common patterns or trends, teams can prioritize potential root causes and develop targeted strategies for addressing underlying issues.

Furthermore, organizations may use techniques such as Failure Mode and Effects Analysis (FMEA) or Fault Tree Analysis (FTA) to systematically evaluate the potential failure modes and consequences within a system or process and identify critical points of failure. FMEA involves identifying potential failure modes within a system, analyzing their potential effects, and prioritizing them based on severity, frequency, and detectability. FTA, on the other hand, involves constructing a logical diagram of all possible combinations of events that could lead to a particular failure and analyzing the probability and consequences of each event.

To perform FMEA or FTA, teams may use specialized software or tools that provide features such as risk assessment matrices, failure mode libraries, and automated calculations. Alternatively, they may use manual methods such as spreadsheets or diagrams to document potential failure modes, consequences, and mitigation strategies. By systematically analyzing potential failure modes and their effects, teams can identify critical points of failure and implement preventive measures to reduce the likelihood of incidents occurring.

In summary, Root Cause Analysis (RCA) Techniques are essential tools for ITSM professionals, enabling them to identify underlying causes of incidents and problems within the IT environment and implement effective solutions to prevent recurrence. By leveraging techniques such as the "5 Whys" method, Fishbone Diagrams, statistical analysis, and failure mode analysis, organizations can systematically investigate and analyze incidents, identify root causes, and develop targeted strategies for addressing underlying issues. By addressing root causes and implementing preventive measures, organizations can improve service reliability, minimize downtime, and enhance customer satisfaction. Proactive Problem Management Strategies are essential components of IT Service Management (ITSM), aimed at identifying and addressing the underlying causes of recurring incidents and problems within the IT environment before they escalate into major disruptions. Unlike reactive problem management, which focuses on resolving incidents as they occur, proactive problem management takes a proactive approach to prevent incidents from happening in the first place by identifying patterns, trends, and underlying issues that may lead to recurring problems.

One proactive problem management strategy is the implementation of Trend Analysis, which involves analyzing historical incident data to identify recurring patterns or trends that may indicate underlying systemic issues. By analyzing incident data over time, ITSM professionals can identify commonalities among incidents, such as recurring error messages, similar symptoms, or common root causes, and prioritize them for further investigation and analysis.

To perform trend analysis, ITSM professionals can use statistical analysis tools or built-in reporting features within ITSM software to generate reports and visualizations of incident data over time. For example, they may use tools such as Microsoft Excel or Tableau to create charts, graphs, and dashboards that illustrate trends in incident volume, frequency, and severity. By analyzing these trends, teams can identify areas of the IT environment that may be prone to recurring problems and develop targeted strategies for addressing underlying issues.

Another proactive problem management strategy is the implementation of Root Cause Analysis (RCA) techniques, which involve investigating and analyzing the underlying causes of incidents and problems to identify and address their root causes. RCA techniques such as the "5 Whys" method, Fishbone Diagrams, and Failure Mode and Effects Analysis (FMEA) can help ITSM professionals systematically uncover the underlying factors contributing to recurring problems and develop targeted solutions to prevent their recurrence.

To perform RCA, ITSM professionals can use a combination of manual and automated techniques to investigate incidents, gather data, and analyze root causes. For example, they may conduct interviews with stakeholders, review incident reports and documentation, and analyze system logs and diagnostic data to identify potential contributing factors. Additionally, they may use specialized RCA software or tools that provide features such as root cause libraries, fault tree diagrams, and automated workflows to facilitate the RCA process.

Furthermore, organizations may implement Problem Management Workshops or Kaizen Events, which bring together cross-functional teams and stakeholders to collaboratively identify and address underlying issues within the IT environment. These workshops typically involve facilitated brainstorming sessions, root cause analysis exercises, and action planning activities aimed at developing targeted solutions to prevent the recurrence of problems.

To conduct problem management workshops, organizations can use facilitation techniques such as brainstorming, affinity diagramming, and cause-and-effect analysis to encourage participation and collaboration among team members. Additionally, they may use collaborative tools such as virtual whiteboards, online forums, and video conferencing platforms to facilitate remote participation and engagement.

Moreover, organizations may implement Continuous Improvement Programs or Lean Six Sigma methodologies, which provide structured frameworks for identifying, prioritizing, and addressing process inefficiencies and improvement opportunities within the IT environment. These methodologies emphasize the importance of data-driven decision-making, root cause analysis, and continuous monitoring and improvement to drive ongoing performance improvement and prevent the recurrence of problems.

To implement Continuous Improvement Programs or Lean Six Sigma methodologies, organizations can establish cross-functional improvement teams, define key performance indicators (KPIs) and metrics for measuring performance, and implement structured improvement cycles such as Plan-Do-Check-Act (PDCA) or Define-Measure-Analyze-Improve-Control (DMAIC). By leveraging these methodologies, organizations can systematically identify and address underlying issues within the IT environment, driving continuous improvement and preventing the recurrence of problems. In summary, proactive problem management strategies are essential for preventing recurring incidents and problems within the IT environment. By implementing techniques such as trend analysis, root cause analysis, problem management workshops, and continuous improvement methodologies, organizations can systematically identify and address underlying issues, drive ongoing performance improvement, and enhance the reliability and stability of IT services.

Chapter 7: Change Management Principles

The Change Request Process is a fundamental aspect of IT Service Management (ITSM), providing organizations with a structured framework for managing changes to their IT infrastructure, systems, and services in a controlled and systematic manner. The change request process encompasses a series of steps and procedures designed to assess, authorize, implement, and review changes to the IT environment, ensuring that changes are planned, coordinated, and executed with minimal disruption to business operations and maximum adherence to quality and security standards.

The first step in the change request process is the submission of a Change Request, which is typically initiated by a user, stakeholder, or ITSM professional to propose a change to the IT environment. To submit a change request, users can use a variety of methods, such as filling out an online form, sending an email to the IT service desk, or using a dedicated change management tool or software platform. For example, in a change management tool such as ServiceNow or Jira Service Desk, users may use the "Create New Change Request" feature to fill out a standardized form that includes details such as the nature of the change, the reason for the change, the proposed implementation date, and any associated risks or dependencies.

Once a change request has been submitted, it undergoes a series of evaluation and assessment steps to determine its impact, risk, and feasibility. This typically involves a Change Advisory Board (CAB) or Change Management Team reviewing the change request and assessing its potential impact on the IT environment, business operations, and service levels. To review and evaluate change requests, CAB members may use a combination of qualitative and quantitative criteria, such as the scope of the change, the complexity of the change, the potential risks and benefits, and the availability of resources and expertise.

To facilitate the evaluation and assessment of change requests, organizations may use a structured change assessment process or risk assessment matrix that assigns a risk score to each change request based on predefined criteria. For example, organizations may use a risk assessment matrix that categorizes changes into low, medium, and high-risk categories based on factors such as the potential impact on business operations, the complexity of the change, and the likelihood of success. By using a risk assessment matrix, organizations can prioritize change requests based on their risk level and allocate resources and attention accordingly.

Once a change request has been evaluated and assessed, it undergoes a formal authorization process to approve or reject the change. Authorization typically involves obtaining approval from key stakeholders, such as business owners, department heads, and IT leadership, to ensure that the change is aligned with business objectives, complies with regulatory requirements, and is feasible within the constraints of time, budget, and resources. To obtain authorization for a change request, ITSM professionals may use a change management tool or software platform to route the change request to the appropriate stakeholders for review and approval.

To track and manage change requests throughout the authorization process, organizations may use a change management tool or software platform that provides features such as workflow automation, approval routing, and status tracking. For example, in a change management tool such as ServiceNow or BMC Remedy, change requests may be assigned a status such as "Pending Approval," "Approved," or "Rejected," and automatically routed to the appropriate stakeholders for review and approval. By using a change management tool, organizations can streamline the authorization process, improve accountability and transparency, and ensure that changes are authorized in a timely manner.

Once a change request has been authorized, it undergoes a planning and implementation phase to coordinate the execution of the change within the IT environment. This typically involves developing a detailed implementation plan that outlines the steps, resources, and timelines required to implement the change, as well as any associated risks, dependencies, and contingency plans. To develop an implementation plan, ITSM professionals may use project management techniques such as Work Breakdown Structures (WBS), Gantt charts, and Critical Path Analysis to sequence and schedule tasks, allocate resources, and identify critical milestones and deadlines.

To execute the implementation plan, ITSM professionals may use a combination of manual and automated techniques, depending on the nature and complexity of the change. For example, they may use configuration management tools or scripting languages such as PowerShell or Python to automate the deployment of software updates or configuration changes, ensuring consistency and accuracy across multiple systems and environments. Additionally, they may use manual techniques such as checklist-based procedures or change control boards to coordinate and monitor the execution of the change, ensuring that it is carried out according to plan and in compliance with quality and security standards.

Once the change has been implemented, it undergoes a formal review and evaluation process to assess its effectiveness and impact on the IT environment and business operations. This typically involves conducting a post-implementation review (PIR) or post-mortem analysis to evaluate the success of the change, identify any issues or challenges encountered during the implementation process, and capture lessons learned for future improvements. To conduct a PIR or post-mortem analysis, ITSM professionals may use a structured review process that involves gathering feedback from stakeholders, analyzing performance metrics and key performance indicators (KPIs), and documenting findings and recommendations for future changes.

In summary, the change request process is a critical component of ITSM that provides organizations with a structured framework for managing changes to their IT environment, systems, and services. By following a series of steps and procedures, including change request submission, evaluation and assessment, authorization, planning and implementation, and review and evaluation, organizations can ensure that changes are planned, coordinated, and executed in a controlled and systematic manner, minimizing disruption to business operations and maximizing adherence to quality and security standards.

Change Evaluation and Risk Management are critical components of the Change Management process in IT Service Management (ITSM), aimed at assessing the impact, effectiveness, and potential risks associated with changes to the IT environment, systems, and services. Change evaluation involves analyzing the outcomes and results of implemented changes to determine whether they have achieved their intended objectives and delivered the expected benefits. Risk management, on the other hand, focuses on identifying, assessing, and mitigating potential risks and uncertainties associated with changes, ensuring that they are managed and controlled throughout the change lifecycle.

To effectively evaluate changes, organizations may use Key Performance Indicators (KPIs) and metrics to measure the success and impact of changes on key business and IT objectives. For example, organizations may use metrics such as Mean Time to Repair (MTTR), Mean Time Between Failures (MTBF), and Service Level

Agreement (SLA) compliance to assess the impact of changes on service availability, reliability, and performance. By tracking and analyzing these metrics, organizations can identify trends, patterns, and areas for improvement, enabling them to optimize the change management process and enhance the effectiveness of future changes.

To analyze the outcomes and results of implemented changes, organizations may conduct Post-Implementation Reviews (PIRs) or Post-Mortem Analyses to evaluate the success and effectiveness of changes and identify any issues or challenges encountered during the implementation process. PIRs typically involve gathering feedback from stakeholders, reviewing performance metrics and KPIs, and documenting findings and recommendations for future improvements. By conducting PIRs, organizations can identify lessons learned, best practices, and areas for improvement, enabling them to refine and optimize their change management processes and practices.

Additionally, organizations may use Change Management Software or tools to automate and streamline the change evaluation process, enabling them to capture and analyze data, track and report on key metrics and KPIs, and generate comprehensive reports and dashboards. For example, organizations may use Change Management Software such as ServiceNow or BMC Remedy to track and manage changes, capture feedback and insights from stakeholders, and generate performance reports and analytics to assess the impact and effectiveness of changes.

In addition to change evaluation, organizations must also proactively manage and mitigate potential risks associated with changes to the IT environment. Risk management involves identifying, assessing, and prioritizing potential risks and uncertainties associated with changes, and developing strategies and controls to mitigate or minimize their impact. To effectively manage risks, organizations may use Risk Assessment Techniques such as Risk Matrices, Risk Registers, and Risk Impact Analysis to identify and assess potential risks and their potential impact on business operations and IT services.

Once risks have been identified and assessed, organizations must develop Risk Mitigation Strategies and Controls to address and mitigate potential risks and uncertainties associated with changes. This may involve implementing preventive controls such as change freezes or blackout periods during critical business periods or implementing detective controls such as monitoring and surveillance systems to detect and respond to potential risks and incidents. By developing and implementing risk mitigation strategies and controls, organizations can reduce the likelihood and impact of potential risks associated with changes, ensuring that changes are managed and executed in a controlled and systematic manner.

To effectively manage risks associated with changes, organizations may use Risk Management Software or tools to automate and streamline the risk management process, enabling them to identify, assess, and prioritize risks, develop and implement risk mitigation strategies and controls, and monitor and track risk levels and trends over time. For example, organizations may use Risk Management Software such as RSA Archer or MetricStream to capture and analyze risk data, assess and prioritize risks, and generate risk reports and dashboards to monitor and track risk levels and trends.

Furthermore, organizations may establish a Change Advisory Board (CAB) or Change Management Team to oversee and review changes, assess potential risks, and make informed decisions regarding change authorization and implementation. The CAB typically includes representatives from different stakeholder groups, such as business units, IT departments, and risk management teams, who collaborate to review and assess changes, evaluate potential risks, and make recommendations for change authorization and implementation. By involving stakeholders in the change evaluation and risk management process, organizations can ensure that changes are aligned with business objectives, comply with regulatory requirements, and are implemented in a manner that minimizes disruption and maximizes value.

Overall, change evaluation and risk management are critical components of the change management process in ITSM, enabling organizations to assess the impact, effectiveness, and potential risks associated with changes to the IT environment and ensure that changes are managed and executed in a controlled and systematic manner. By implementing effective change evaluation and risk management practices and leveraging tools and techniques such as KPIs, PIRs, Risk Assessment Techniques, and Risk Management Software, organizations can optimize their change management processes and practices, minimize disruption to business operations, and enhance the value and reliability of IT services.

Chapter 8: Service Level Management Overview

SLA Components and Structure are fundamental aspects of IT Service Management (ITSM), providing organizations with a structured framework for defining, documenting, and managing service level agreements (SLAs) between service providers and customers. SLAs are contractual agreements that outline the agreed-upon levels of service quality, performance, and availability that service providers are expected to deliver to their customers, as well as the consequences for failing to meet these commitments.

The key components of an SLA typically include Service Scope, Service Level Objectives (SLOs), Performance Metrics, Service Credits, and Governance and Reporting mechanisms. Service Scope defines the scope and boundaries of the services covered by the SLA, including the specific services, systems, and applications included in the agreement, as well as any exclusions or limitations. To define the Service Scope of an SLA, organizations may use a combination of qualitative and quantitative criteria, such as business criticality, customer requirements, and service dependencies, to ensure that the SLA accurately reflects the services and expectations of both parties.

Service Level Objectives (SLOs) specify the measurable targets and expectations for service quality, performance, and availability that service providers are contractually obligated to meet. SLOs typically include metrics such as Response Time, Resolution Time, Uptime, and Availability, as well as targets or thresholds for each metric. To define SLOs, organizations may use a combination of historical data, benchmarking, and industry best practices to establish realistic and achievable targets that align with customer expectations and business requirements.

Performance Metrics are quantitative measures used to track and evaluate the performance and effectiveness of service delivery against agreed-upon targets and objectives. Performance metrics may include Key Performance Indicators (KPIs) such as Mean Time to Respond (MTTR), Mean Time to Resolve (MTTR), Service Availability, and Customer Satisfaction, as well as other relevant metrics such as Incident Volume, Service Desk Utilization, and First Call Resolution Rate. To track and monitor performance metrics, organizations may use Monitoring Tools or Performance Management Systems that collect and analyze data from various sources, such as monitoring agents, system logs, and ticketing systems, to provide real-time insights into service performance and availability.

Service Credits are contractual remedies or compensation mechanisms that are triggered when service providers fail to meet their SLA commitments or performance targets. Service credits may take the form of financial penalties, service rebates, or credits towards future services, and are typically calculated based on the severity and duration of the service failure, as well as any predefined escalation or penalty clauses outlined in the SLA. To calculate service credits, organizations may use formulas or calculations based on predefined criteria, such as the percentage of downtime or the number of incidents exceeding the agreed-upon thresholds, to determine the appropriate compensation or penalty amount.

Governance and Reporting mechanisms define the roles, responsibilities, and processes for managing and overseeing the SLA throughout its lifecycle, including SLA Negotiation, Review and Approval, Monitoring and Reporting, and Dispute Resolution. Governance mechanisms may include the establishment of a Service Level Management (SLM) process or function responsible for defining, documenting, and managing SLAs, as well as the creation of a Change Advisory Board (CAB) or SLA Review Board to oversee and review changes to SLAs. To ensure effective governance and reporting, organizations may use SLA Management Tools or Software Platforms that provide features such as SLA Workflow Automation, Reporting Dashboards, and Escalation Management to streamline and automate SLA management processes.

Furthermore, organizations may establish Service Level Agreements (SLA) as part of their IT service delivery to define the expected level of service and support for their customers. To deploy SLAs effectively, organizations may use SLA Management tools or software platforms to define, document, and track SLAs, as well as establish Service Level Agreements (SLA) Templates to standardize and streamline the SLA creation process. For example, organizations may use SLA Management tools such as ServiceNow or BMC

Remedy to define SLAs, specify performance metrics and targets, and establish governance and reporting mechanisms for managing SLAs. By using SLA Management tools and templates, organizations can ensure that SLAs are consistently defined, documented, and managed, and that service providers and customers are held accountable for meeting their SLA commitments and obligations.

In summary, SLA Components and Structure are critical elements of IT Service Management (ITSM) that provide organizations with a structured framework for defining, documenting, and managing service level agreements (SLAs) between service providers and customers. By defining clear and measurable Service Level Objectives (SLOs), establishing performance metrics and targets, implementing governance and reporting mechanisms, and deploying SLA Management tools and templates, organizations can ensure that SLAs are effectively managed and monitored, and that service providers are held accountable for meeting their SLA commitments and obligations.

SLA Monitoring and Review Processes are essential components of IT Service Management (ITSM), providing organizations with mechanisms to track, evaluate, and ensure compliance with service level agreements (SLAs) between service providers and customers. Monitoring and reviewing SLAs involve ongoing assessment of service performance, measurement of key performance indicators (KPIs), identification of deviations from agreed-upon targets, and implementation of corrective actions to address deficiencies and improve service delivery. These processes are crucial for maintaining service quality, meeting customer expectations, and fostering transparency and accountability in service delivery.

To effectively monitor SLAs, organizations use Monitoring Tools or Performance Management Systems to collect, analyze, and report on relevant performance data and metrics. These tools allow organizations to track the performance of IT services in real-time, identify trends and patterns, and generate reports and dashboards to communicate performance to stakeholders. For example, organizations may use monitoring tools such as Nagios, Zabbix, or Prometheus to monitor service availability, response times, and other performance metrics, and alert administrators to potential issues or breaches of SLAs.

Additionally, organizations may implement Service Level Management (SLM) processes or functions responsible for overseeing the monitoring and review of SLAs. SLM processes define roles, responsibilities, and procedures for monitoring SLAs, establishing escalation paths for addressing breaches or deviations, and conducting regular reviews and assessments of service performance. These processes ensure that SLAs are actively managed and that corrective actions are taken promptly to address any deviations or deficiencies in service delivery.

To monitor SLAs effectively, organizations use Key Performance Indicators (KPIs) and Service Level Objectives (SLOs) to measure and evaluate service performance against agreed-upon targets and objectives. KPIs are quantitative measures used to assess the performance and effectiveness of IT services, while SLOs are specific, measurable targets for service quality, availability, and performance. For example, organizations may use KPIs such as Mean Time to Respond (MTTR), Mean Time to Resolve (MTTR), and Service Availability to measure the performance of their IT services and evaluate compliance with SLAs.

To review SLAs, organizations conduct regular SLA Review Meetings or Service Reviews to assess service performance, identify areas for improvement, and address any issues or concerns raised by stakeholders. These meetings typically involve representatives from both the service provider and customer sides, including service owners, IT managers, and business stakeholders, who collaborate to review performance data, discuss service levels, and make recommendations for improvement. During these meetings, organizations may use SLA Reports and Dashboards to present performance data, trends, and analysis, and facilitate discussion and decision-making.

Furthermore, organizations use SLA Management Tools or Software Platforms to automate and streamline the SLA monitoring and review process, enabling them to track SLA performance, generate performance reports and dashboards, and manage SLA compliance efficiently. These tools provide features such as SLA Workflow Automation, Performance Monitoring, and Reporting Dashboards to facilitate the monitoring and review of SLAs. For example, organizations may use SLA management tools such as ServiceNow or BMC Remedy to define SLAs, track performance metrics, and generate SLA performance reports and dashboards.

To deploy SLA monitoring and review processes effectively, organizations must establish clear roles, responsibilities, and procedures for managing SLAs, including defining SLA targets and objectives, monitoring performance metrics, conducting regular reviews and assessments, and implementing corrective actions as needed. By implementing robust SLA monitoring and review processes and leveraging monitoring tools and SLA management software, organizations can ensure that SLAs are actively managed, service performance is monitored effectively, and corrective actions are taken promptly to address any deviations or deficiencies in service delivery.

Chapter 9: ITIL Best Practices for Service Desk Operations

Service Desk Performance Metrics play a crucial role in evaluating the efficiency, effectiveness, and quality of service desk operations in IT Service Management (ITSM). These metrics provide valuable insights into the performance of the service desk team, the responsiveness to user requests and incidents, and the overall customer satisfaction levels. By measuring and analyzing key performance indicators (KPIs), organizations can identify areas for improvement, optimize service delivery processes, and enhance the overall service desk performance.

One of the fundamental metrics used to evaluate service desk performance is First Call Resolution (FCR) rate. FCR measures the percentage of incidents or service requests that are resolved by the service desk on the first contact with the user. A higher FCR rate indicates that the service desk team is capable of resolving issues efficiently and effectively, reducing the need for escalations and improving user satisfaction. To calculate the FCR rate, organizations can use the following CLI command:

mathematicaCopy code

```
FCR = (Number of incidents resolved on first contact / Total number of incidents) * 100
```

Another important metric is Mean Time to Resolve (MTTR), which measures the average time it takes for the service desk to resolve incidents or service requests. A lower MTTR indicates that the service desk team is able to address issues promptly and minimize downtime, thereby improving user productivity and satisfaction. To calculate the MTTR, organizations can use the following CLI command:

cssCopy code

MTTR = (Total time to resolve all incidents / Number of incidents resolved)

Additionally, organizations may track and monitor Service Level Agreement (SLA) compliance as a performance metric for the service desk. SLA compliance measures the percentage of incidents or service requests that are resolved within the agreed-upon SLA targets. By monitoring SLA compliance, organizations can ensure that service desk operations are meeting the expectations and commitments outlined in SLAs, thereby enhancing customer satisfaction and maintaining service quality. To calculate SLA compliance, organizations can use the following CLI command:

mathematicaCopy code

SLA Compliance = (Number of incidents resolved within SLA / Total number of incidents) * 100

Moreover, organizations may track Customer Satisfaction (CSAT) scores as a metric to gauge the level of satisfaction among users with the service desk support experience. CSAT scores are typically obtained through user surveys or feedback mechanisms and provide valuable insights into user perceptions of service desk responsiveness, professionalism, and effectiveness. By monitoring CSAT scores, organizations can identify areas for improvement and prioritize initiatives to enhance customer satisfaction. To calculate CSAT scores, organizations can use the following CLI command:

mathematicaCopy code

CSAT Score = (Number of satisfied responses / Total number of responses) * 100

Furthermore, organizations may track and analyze Average Speed of Answer (ASA) as a performance metric for the service desk. ASA measures the average time it takes for the service desk to answer incoming calls or respond to incoming emails or chat messages. A lower ASA indicates that the service desk team is able to handle user inquiries and requests promptly, reducing wait times and improving user satisfaction. To calculate ASA, organizations can use the following CLI command:

cssCopy code

ASA = (Total time taken to answer all calls / Total number of calls answered)

Additionally, organizations may monitor and analyze Call Abandonment Rate (CAR) as a metric to assess the efficiency of the service desk in handling incoming calls. CAR measures the percentage of calls that are abandoned by users before reaching a service desk agent. A lower CAR indicates that the service desk team is able to manage call volumes effectively and minimize wait times, thereby improving user experience and satisfaction. To calculate CAR, organizations can use the following CLI command:

mathematicaCopy code

CAR = (Number of abandoned calls / Total number of incoming calls) * 100

Moreover, organizations may track and analyze Incident Volume as a performance metric for the service desk. Incident Volume measures the total number of incidents or service requests handled by the service desk within a specific time period. By monitoring Incident Volume, organizations can identify trends, patterns, and peaks in workload, and allocate resources and staffing accordingly to ensure timely and efficient service delivery. To calculate Incident Volume, organizations can use the following CLI command:

mathematicaCopy code

Incident Volume = Total number of incidents or service requests

Furthermore, organizations may monitor and analyze Service Desk Utilization as a metric to assess the efficiency of resource utilization within the service desk team. Service Desk Utilization measures the percentage of time that service desk agents spend actively handling user inquiries and requests. By optimizing Service Desk Utilization, organizations can ensure that service desk resources are utilized effectively and efficiently, minimizing idle time and maximizing productivity. To calculate Service Desk Utilization, organizations can use the following CLI command:

cssCopy code

Service Desk Utilization = (Total time spent on active service desk activities / Total available time) * 100

In summary, Service Desk Performance Metrics are essential for evaluating the efficiency, effectiveness, and quality of service desk operations in ITSM. By tracking and analyzing key performance indicators such as First Call Resolution rate, Mean Time to Resolve, SLA compliance, Customer Satisfaction scores, Average Speed of Answer, Call Abandonment Rate, Incident Volume, and Service Desk Utilization, organizations can identify areas for improvement, optimize service delivery processes, and enhance overall service desk performance.

Continual Service Improvement (CSI) is a fundamental aspect of IT Service Management (ITSM) that focuses on enhancing the quality, efficiency, and effectiveness of service delivery processes over time. CSI involves the systematic review, analysis, and evaluation of service desk operations to identify areas for improvement and implement initiatives to drive ongoing enhancements. By adopting a proactive approach to CSI, service desk teams can optimize service delivery, improve user satisfaction, and align IT services with business objectives.

To initiate the CSI process for the service desk, organizations may start by conducting a Service Desk Assessment to evaluate the current state of service desk operations and identify areas for improvement. This assessment may involve gathering data and feedback from stakeholders, analyzing performance metrics and KPIs, and conducting interviews or surveys to understand user expectations and pain points. By assessing the current state of the service desk, organizations can identify strengths, weaknesses, opportunities, and threats, and develop a roadmap for implementing CSI initiatives.

One technique used in CSI is the Plan-Do-Check-Act (PDCA) cycle, also known as the Deming Cycle or the Shewhart Cycle. The PDCA cycle is a systematic approach to continuous improvement that involves four key steps: Plan, Do, Check, and Act. In the Plan phase, organizations identify improvement opportunities, set objectives, and develop action plans to address identified issues or gaps. In the Do phase, organizations implement the planned improvements and initiatives. In the Check phase, organizations monitor and evaluate the results of the implemented changes, measure performance against objectives, and identify any deviations or areas for further improvement. Finally, in the Act phase, organizations take corrective actions based on the findings from the Check phase, adjust plans and processes as needed, and continue the cycle of improvement.

To deploy the PDCA cycle for CSI, organizations may use the following CLI commands or techniques:

Plan: Identify improvement opportunities and set objectives.

perlCopy code

```
$ grep -i "improvement opportunities" service_desk_assessment.txt
```

shellCopy code

```
$ echo "Set objectives for improvement initiatives."
```

Do: Implement planned improvements and initiatives.

cssCopy code

```
$       ansible-playbook      -i       inventory_file
csi_improvement_playbook.yml
```

Check: Monitor and evaluate the results of the implemented changes.

```shell
shellCopy code
$ tail -n 1000 service_desk_performance_logs.txt
```

```ruby
rubyCopy code
$   curl   -X   GET   http://service-desk-metrics-
api.com/check
```

Act: Take corrective actions based on the findings from the Check phase.

```ruby
rubyCopy code
$       sed       -i       's/old_value/new_value/g'
service_desk_configuration_file.txt
```

```ruby
rubyCopy code
$ systemctl restart service_desk_service
```

Another technique used in CSI is the use of Key Performance Indicators (KPIs) to measure and monitor the performance of service desk operations. KPIs are quantifiable metrics used to evaluate the success and effectiveness of service delivery processes. Common KPIs used for service desk CSI include First Call Resolution (FCR) rate, Mean Time to Resolve (MTTR), Customer Satisfaction (CSAT) scores, and Service Level Agreement (SLA) compliance. By tracking and analyzing KPIs, organizations can identify trends, patterns, and areas for improvement, and make data-driven decisions to optimize service desk performance.

To deploy KPIs for CSI, organizations may use the following CLI commands or techniques:

Define KPIs: Identify relevant KPIs based on organizational objectives and priorities.

shellCopy code

```
$ echo "Define KPIs for service desk CSI."
```

rubyCopy code

```
$ vi kpi_definitions.txt
```

Collect Data: Gather data and metrics related to the defined KPIs.

perlCopy code

```
$ grep -i "kpi_name" service_desk_performance_logs.txt
```

rubyCopy code

```
$ curl -X GET http://service-desk-metrics-api.com/kpi_data
```

Analyze Data: Analyze collected data to identify trends, patterns, and areas for improvement.

rubyCopy code

```
$ python analyze_kpi_data.py
```

Implement Improvements: Based on the analysis, implement initiatives to address identified areas for improvement.

cssCopy code

```
$ ansible-playbook -i inventory_file kpi_improvement_playbook.yml
```

In addition to the PDCA cycle and KPIs, organizations may also leverage tools and frameworks such as Lean Six Sigma, ITIL (Information Technology Infrastructure Library), and ISO/IEC 20000 to drive CSI initiatives for the service desk. These methodologies provide structured approaches and best practices for process improvement, problem-solving, and performance optimization. By adopting these frameworks, organizations can streamline service desk operations, eliminate waste, and deliver value-added services to customers.

Overall, Continual Service Improvement is a critical aspect of service desk operations in ITSM, enabling organizations to drive ongoing enhancements, optimize performance, and deliver superior services to users. By deploying techniques such as the PDCA cycle, KPIs, and leveraging tools and frameworks, organizations can establish a culture of continuous improvement and ensure that service desk operations evolve to meet the changing needs and expectations of customers and stakeholders.

Chapter 10: Implementing ITIL 4 Standard in Your Organization

Planning and Preparation for ITIL Implementation are crucial stages in adopting the ITIL (Information Technology Infrastructure Library) framework within an organization. This process involves thorough assessment, strategic planning, stakeholder engagement, and resource allocation to ensure successful implementation and alignment with business objectives. The first step in planning for ITIL implementation is to conduct a comprehensive assessment of the organization's current IT service management practices, processes, and capabilities. This assessment helps identify areas of strength, weaknesses, gaps, and opportunities for improvement, laying the foundation for a targeted and effective ITIL implementation strategy.

To conduct the assessment, organizations may use various assessment tools, frameworks, and methodologies such as ITIL self-assessment questionnaires, maturity models, and benchmarking studies. These tools help gather data, feedback, and insights from stakeholders across the organization, including IT teams, business units, and end-users, to understand current challenges, pain points, and priorities. By analyzing the assessment findings, organizations can identify key areas for improvement and develop a roadmap for ITIL implementation that addresses specific organizational needs and objectives.

Once the assessment is complete, the next step is to define the scope and objectives of the ITIL implementation initiative. This involves setting clear goals, timelines, and success criteria for the implementation project, as well as defining the scope of ITIL processes and practices to be implemented. Organizations may use the ITIL framework itself as a reference for defining the scope, selecting relevant ITIL processes and practices based on organizational priorities and requirements. Additionally, organizations may leverage industry best practices, standards, and guidelines to inform their ITIL implementation strategy and ensure alignment with industry norms and expectations.

To define the scope and objectives of the ITIL implementation initiative, organizations may use the following CLI commands or techniques:

Define project scope:

shellCopy code

```
$ echo "Define scope of ITIL implementation project."
```

rubyCopy code

```
$ vi itil_implementation_scope.txt
```

Set project objectives:

shellCopy code

```
$ echo "Set objectives for ITIL implementation project."
```

rubyCopy code

```
$ vi itil_implementation_objectives.txt
```

Develop implementation roadmap:

cssCopy code

```
$        ansible-playbook       -i        inventory_file
itil_implementation_playbook.yml
```

Identify key stakeholders:

perlCopy code

```
$ grep -i "stakeholders" itil_assessment_report.txt
```

shellCopy code

```
$ curl -X GET http://itil_stakeholder_registry.com
```

Establish communication plan:

shellCopy code

```
$ echo "Develop communication plan for ITIL
implementation."
```

rubyCopy code

```
$ vi itil_implementation_communication_plan.txt
```

Once the scope and objectives are defined, organizations need to engage key stakeholders and secure buy-in and support for the ITIL implementation initiative. This involves communicating the benefits, objectives, and expected outcomes of the ITIL implementation to stakeholders across the organization, including senior management, IT teams, business units, and end-users. By engaging stakeholders early in the process and involving them in decision-making and planning, organizations can build consensus, foster collaboration, and ensure alignment of ITIL implementation efforts with organizational goals and priorities.

To engage stakeholders and secure buy-in for the ITIL implementation initiative, organizations may use the following CLI commands or techniques:

Identify key stakeholders:

perlCopy code

```
$ grep -i "key stakeholders" itil_assessment_report.txt
```

shellCopy code

```
$ curl -X GET http://itil_stakeholder_registry.com
```

Develop stakeholder engagement plan:

shellCopy code

```
$ echo "Develop stakeholder engagement plan for ITIL implementation."
```

rubyCopy code

```
$                                              vi
itil_implementation_stakeholder_engagement_plan.txt
```

Conduct stakeholder meetings and workshops:

cssCopy code

```
$       ansible-playbook     -i       inventory_file
stakeholder_engagement_workshop_playbook.yml
```

Present ITIL implementation roadmap and benefits:

shellCopy code

```
$ echo "Present ITIL implementation roadmap and benefits to stakeholders."
```

rubyCopy code

```
$ vi itil_implementation_presentation.txt
```

In addition to engaging stakeholders, organizations need to allocate sufficient resources, including budget, manpower, and technology, to support the ITIL implementation initiative. This may involve securing funding and budget approvals, recruiting and training staff, and investing in ITIL-related tools, technologies, and infrastructure. By allocating adequate resources and ensuring proper resourcing and staffing for the ITIL implementation project, organizations can mitigate risks, overcome challenges, and ensure successful implementation and adoption of ITIL practices and processes.

To allocate resources for the ITIL implementation initiative, organizations may use the following CLI commands or techniques:

Secure funding and budget approvals:

shellCopy code

```
$ echo "Secure funding and budget approvals for ITIL implementation project."
```

rubyCopy code

```
$ vi itil_implementation_budget_request.txt
```

Recruit and train staff:

cssCopy code

```
$ ansible-playbook -i inventory_file staff_training_playbook.yml
```

Invest in ITIL-related tools and technologies:

shellCopy code

```
$ echo "Invest in ITIL-related tools and technologies for ITIL implementation."
```

rubyCopy code

```
$ vi itil_implementation_technology_plan.txt
```

Establish project governance and oversight:

perlCopy code

```
$ grep -i "project governance" itil_implementation_strategy.txt
```

shellCopy code

```
$ curl -X GET http://itil_implementation_dashboard.com
```

By following a structured approach to planning and preparation for ITIL implementation, organizations can lay the groundwork for a successful and sustainable ITIL implementation initiative. Through thorough assessment, strategic planning, stakeholder engagement, and resource allocation, organizations can ensure that their ITIL implementation efforts are well-planned, well-executed, and well-aligned with organizational goals and objectives.

ITIL (Information Technology Infrastructure Library) Adoption Challenges and Solutions are critical aspects for organizations embarking on the journey to implement ITIL practices and frameworks. While ITIL offers numerous benefits such as improved service quality, enhanced customer satisfaction, and increased operational efficiency, organizations often encounter various challenges during the adoption process. These challenges may arise from factors such as organizational culture, resistance to change, lack of awareness or understanding of ITIL, and resource constraints. However, by recognizing these challenges and implementing appropriate solutions, organizations can overcome barriers to ITIL adoption and achieve successful implementation and integration of ITIL practices into their operations.

One of the primary challenges organizations face during ITIL adoption is resistance to change from stakeholders across the organization. Resistance to change may stem from fear of the unknown, skepticism about the benefits of ITIL, or concerns about disruptions to existing processes and workflows. To address this challenge, organizations need to foster a culture of openness, transparency, and collaboration, and communicate the benefits and rationale behind ITIL adoption to stakeholders effectively. Additionally, organizations can involve key stakeholders in the decision-making process, seek their input and feedback, and address their concerns and objections through education, training, and awareness-building initiatives.

To address resistance to change during ITIL adoption, organizations may use the following CLI commands or techniques:

Identify stakeholders:

perlCopy code

```
$ grep -i "key stakeholders" itil_adoption_plan.txt
```

shellCopy code

```
$ curl -X GET http://stakeholder_registry.com
```

Conduct stakeholder engagement sessions:

cssCopy code

```
$ ansible-playbook -i inventory_file stakeholder_engagement_playbook .yml
```

Communicate benefits of ITIL adoption:

shellCopy code

```
$ echo "Communicate benefits of ITIL adoption to stakeholders."
```

rubyCopy code

```
$ vi itil_adoption_benefits_communication_plan.txt
```

Another common challenge organizations encounter during ITIL adoption is the lack of awareness or understanding of ITIL practices and frameworks among staff. Many employees may be unfamiliar with ITIL concepts, terminology, and best practices, which can hinder adoption and implementation efforts. To address this challenge, organizations need to invest in education, training, and skill development initiatives to build ITIL competency and capability among staff. This may involve providing ITIL training courses, workshops, and certification programs to employees, as well as offering resources such as manuals, guides, and online tutorials to support self-directed learning and knowledge acquisition.

To address the lack of awareness or understanding of ITIL among staff, organizations may use the following CLI commands or techniques:

Develop ITIL training curriculum:

shellCopy code

```
$ echo "Develop ITIL training curriculum for staff."
```

rubyCopy code

```
$ vi itil_training_curriculum.txt
```

Schedule ITIL training sessions:

cssCopy code

```
$ ansible-playbook -i inventory_file itil_training_playbook.yml
```

Provide access to ITIL resources:

shellCopy code

```
$ mkdir itil_resources
```

shellCopy code

```
$ wget http://itil_guide.com -O itil_guide.pdf
```

Resource constraints are another significant challenge organizations face during ITIL adoption. Implementing

ITIL practices and frameworks often requires investments in technology, tools, and infrastructure, as well as dedicating time, manpower, and financial resources to training, education, and implementation activities. However, limited budgets, competing priorities, and competing initiatives may constrain organizations' ability to allocate sufficient resources for ITIL adoption. To address this challenge, organizations need to prioritize ITIL adoption initiatives based on their potential impact and return on investment, and seek creative solutions to optimize resource utilization and minimize costs.

To address resource constraints during ITIL adoption, organizations may use the following CLI commands or techniques:

Prioritize ITIL adoption initiatives:

shellCopy code

```
$ echo "Prioritize ITIL adoption initiatives based on ROI and impact."
```

rubyCopy code

```
$ vi itil_adoption_prioritization_matrix.txt
```

Allocate budget for ITIL adoption:

shellCopy code

```
$ echo "Allocate budget for ITIL adoption initiatives."
```

rubyCopy code

```
$ vi itil_adoption_budget_allocation_plan.txt
```

Optimize resource utilization:

perlCopy code

```
$ grep -i "resource optimization" itil_adoption_strategy.txt
```

```shell
shellCopy code
$                curl              -X              GET
http://resource_utilization_dashboard.com
```

Furthermore, organizations may encounter challenges related to integrating ITIL practices and frameworks into existing processes, workflows, and systems. Legacy systems, siloed departments, and disparate tools and technologies may pose obstacles to seamless integration and interoperability, leading to inefficiencies and inconsistencies in service delivery. To address this challenge, organizations need to conduct a thorough assessment of existing processes and systems, identify integration points and dependencies, and develop a roadmap for integrating ITIL practices into the existing IT ecosystem. This may involve implementing interoperability standards, integrating ITIL-compatible tools and technologies, and redesigning workflows and processes to align with ITIL best practices.

To address integration challenges during ITIL adoption, organizations may use the following CLI commands or techniques:

Assess existing processes and systems:

```perl
perlCopy code
$     grep     -i     "existing     systems"
itil_integration_assessment.txt
```

```shell
shellCopy code
$ curl -X GET http://existing_systems_inventory.com
```

Identify integration points and dependencies:

```perl
perlCopy code
```

```shell
$ grep -i "integration points" itil_integration_assessment.txt
```
shellCopy code
```shell
$ curl -X GET http://integration_dependencies_registry.com
```
Develop integration roadmap:

shellCopy code
```shell
$ echo "Develop roadmap for integrating ITIL practices into existing processes."
```
rubyCopy code
```ruby
$ vi itil_integration_roadmap.txt
```
Implement ITIL-compatible tools and technologies:

cssCopy code
```css
$ ansible-playbook -i inventory_file itil_integration_playbook.yml
```
By recognizing and addressing these challenges through strategic planning, stakeholder engagement, education and training, resource allocation, and integration efforts, organizations can overcome barriers to ITIL adoption and achieve successful implementation and integration of ITIL practices and frameworks. Through perseverance, collaboration, and continuous improvement, organizations can unlock the full potential of ITIL to enhance service quality, drive operational excellence, and deliver value to customers and stakeholders.

BOOK 2
MASTERING KPIS
OPTIMIZING SERVICE DESK PERFORMANCE

ROB BOTWRIGHT

Chapter 1: Understanding Key Performance Indicators (KPIs)

The importance of Key Performance Indicators (KPIs) in Service Desk Management cannot be overstated. KPIs serve as critical metrics that enable organizations to assess the performance, efficiency, and effectiveness of their service desk operations. By measuring key aspects of service desk performance, KPIs provide valuable insights into areas of strength, weakness, and improvement opportunities, allowing organizations to make informed decisions, drive continuous improvement, and enhance service delivery to meet customer expectations and business objectives.

KPIs play a pivotal role in monitoring and evaluating service desk performance across various dimensions, including response times, resolution rates, customer satisfaction levels, and adherence to service level agreements (SLAs). These metrics provide quantitative data that enable organizations to assess the effectiveness of their service desk processes, identify bottlenecks and inefficiencies, and prioritize areas for improvement. By tracking KPIs over time, organizations can measure progress, benchmark performance against industry standards, and set targets for continuous improvement.

To effectively leverage KPIs in service desk management, organizations need to define relevant and meaningful metrics that align with their business objectives and priorities. This involves identifying key service desk processes, activities, and outcomes that directly impact service quality, customer satisfaction, and operational efficiency. Once KPIs are defined, organizations need to establish clear measurement criteria, data collection methods, and reporting mechanisms to ensure consistent and accurate tracking of performance metrics.

Common KPIs used in service desk management include:

First Call Resolution (FCR) Rate: This metric measures the percentage of incidents or service requests resolved on the first contact with the service desk. A high FCR rate indicates efficient and effective problem resolution, reducing the need for multiple interactions and minimizing customer inconvenience.

Mean Time to Resolve (MTTR): MTTR measures the average time it takes to resolve incidents or service requests from the time they are reported to the time they are resolved. A lower MTTR indicates faster resolution times and improved service desk responsiveness.

Customer Satisfaction (CSAT) Scores: CSAT scores measure customer satisfaction levels with the service desk's performance and responsiveness. By collecting feedback from customers through surveys or feedback forms, organizations can gauge customer perceptions and identify areas for improvement.

Service Level Agreement (SLA) Compliance: SLA compliance measures the extent to which the service desk meets the agreed-upon service levels and response times defined in SLAs. Tracking SLA compliance ensures accountability and adherence to service commitments, fostering trust and confidence among customers and stakeholders.

To track and analyze KPIs effectively, organizations may use various tools and technologies, including service desk software, performance monitoring systems, and business intelligence platforms. These tools provide capabilities for data collection, aggregation, analysis, and visualization, enabling organizations to gain actionable insights into service desk performance and make data-driven decisions to drive continuous improvement.

One example of a CLI command used for tracking KPIs is: perlCopy code

```
$    grep    -i    "first    call    resolution"
service_desk_performance_logs.txt
```

This command searches the service desk performance logs for instances of first call resolution, allowing organizations to measure the frequency and effectiveness of this key metric.

In addition to tracking KPIs internally, organizations may also benchmark their performance against industry standards and best practices to identify areas for improvement and drive performance excellence. Benchmarking allows organizations to compare their performance metrics with those of peer organizations or industry benchmarks, gaining insights into leading practices and identifying opportunities for innovation and optimization.

Overall, KPIs play a central role in service desk management by providing organizations with objective, measurable data to assess performance, identify improvement opportunities, and drive continuous improvement. By defining relevant metrics, implementing robust measurement mechanisms, and leveraging tools and technologies for analysis and reporting, organizations can optimize service desk operations, enhance customer satisfaction, and achieve their business goals and objectives.

Types and categories of Key Performance Indicators (KPIs) encompass a diverse range of metrics used to measure and evaluate performance across various aspects of business operations. KPIs are essential tools that enable organizations to assess their progress toward strategic objectives, identify areas for improvement, and drive performance excellence. These metrics can be classified into several broad categories based on their focus areas, including financial, operational, customer, and employee-related KPIs. Within each category, there are multiple types of KPIs that organizations can track to monitor performance and make informed decisions.

Financial KPIs are metrics that measure the financial performance and health of an organization. These KPIs provide insights into revenue generation, profitability, cost management, and overall financial stability. Examples of financial KPIs include:

Revenue Growth Rate: This metric measures the percentage increase in revenue over a specific period, indicating the organization's ability to generate more income over time.

Profit Margin: Profit margin measures the percentage of revenue that represents profit after deducting expenses. A higher profit margin indicates better profitability and financial health.

Return on Investment (ROI): ROI measures the return generated from an investment relative to its cost. It helps assess the efficiency and effectiveness of investment decisions.

Cash Flow: Cash flow measures the movement of cash into and out of the organization over a specific period, reflecting liquidity and financial stability.

Operational KPIs focus on measuring the efficiency and effectiveness of business processes and operations. These metrics help organizations optimize workflows, reduce costs, and improve productivity. Examples of operational KPIs include:

Cycle Time: Cycle time measures the time it takes to complete a specific process or task from start to finish. It helps identify bottlenecks and inefficiencies in operational workflows.

Production Output: Production output measures the quantity of goods or services produced by the organization within a given period, reflecting production efficiency and capacity utilization.

Inventory Turnover: Inventory turnover measures the number of times inventory is sold or used within a specific period, indicating how effectively inventory is managed and utilized.

On-Time Delivery Rate: On-time delivery rate measures the percentage of orders or deliveries completed on time as promised to customers, reflecting reliability and service quality.

Customer KPIs focus on measuring customer satisfaction, loyalty, and engagement with the organization's products or services. These metrics help organizations understand customer needs, preferences, and behaviors to deliver exceptional customer experiences. Examples of customer KPIs include:

Net Promoter Score (NPS): NPS measures customer loyalty and satisfaction by asking customers how likely they are to recommend the organization to others. It helps assess overall customer sentiment and brand advocacy.

Customer Satisfaction Score (CSAT): CSAT measures customer satisfaction with a specific interaction, transaction, or experience with the organization. It provides immediate feedback on service quality and customer experience.

Customer Retention Rate: Customer retention rate measures the percentage of customers retained over a specific period, indicating customer loyalty and long-term value.

Customer Lifetime Value (CLV): CLV measures the total revenue generated from a customer over their entire relationship with the organization, helping prioritize high-value customers and tailor marketing strategies accordingly.

Employee-related KPIs focus on measuring employee performance, engagement, and satisfaction within the organization. These metrics help organizations assess workforce productivity, morale, and retention. Examples of employee-related KPIs include:

Employee Turnover Rate: Employee turnover rate measures the percentage of employees who leave the organization within a specific period, indicating workforce stability and retention efforts.

Employee Satisfaction Index: Employee satisfaction index measures employee satisfaction and engagement with their work, team, and organization. It helps identify areas for improvement in the work environment and culture.

Training and Development Hours: Training and development hours measure the amount of time employees spend on training and professional development activities, reflecting investment in employee growth and skills enhancement.

Employee Performance Ratings: Employee performance ratings assess individual performance against established goals and objectives, providing feedback for performance improvement and development planning.

To track and analyze KPIs effectively, organizations can use various tools and techniques, including data analytics software, dashboards, and performance management systems. These tools enable organizations to collect, visualize, and interpret KPI data in real-time, facilitating informed decision-making and continuous improvement efforts.

Overall, types and categories of KPIs provide organizations with valuable insights into their performance across different dimensions of business operations. By tracking and monitoring relevant KPIs, organizations can identify strengths, weaknesses, and improvement opportunities, driving performance excellence and achieving strategic objectives.

Chapter 2: Identifying Relevant KPIs for Service Desk Performance

Selection criteria for Service Desk Key Performance Indicators (KPIs) are essential considerations that organizations must take into account when determining which metrics to track and measure to evaluate the performance of their service desk operations. These criteria help organizations identify relevant, meaningful, and actionable KPIs that align with their business objectives, service level agreements (SLAs), and customer expectations. By selecting the right KPIs, organizations can gain valuable insights into service desk performance, drive continuous improvement, and deliver exceptional customer service.

The first selection criterion for Service Desk KPIs is relevance to business objectives and priorities. Organizations need to align KPIs with their strategic goals, mission, and vision to ensure that they measure outcomes that are directly linked to overall organizational success. KPIs should focus on areas that are critical to achieving business objectives, such as customer satisfaction, service quality, and operational efficiency. By selecting KPIs that are relevant to business objectives, organizations can ensure that their service desk efforts contribute to broader organizational goals and priorities.

To ensure relevance to business objectives, organizations may use the following CLI commands or techniques:

Define organizational goals:

shellCopy code

```
$ echo "Define organizational goals and objectives."
```
rubyCopy code
```
$ vi organizational_goals.txt
```
Identify key performance areas:
perlCopy code
```
$ grep -i "key performance areas" organizational_strategy.txt
```
shellCopy code
```
$ curl -X GET http://key_performance_areas_registry.com
```
Align KPIs with business objectives:
shellCopy code
```
$ echo "Align Service Desk KPIs with organizational goals and priorities."
```
rubyCopy code
```
$ vi service_desk_kpi_alignment_plan.txt
```

The second selection criterion for Service Desk KPIs is measurability and quantifiability. KPIs should be measurable using objective, quantitative data to enable accurate tracking and analysis of performance over time. Measurable KPIs allow organizations to monitor progress, set targets, and benchmark performance against industry standards and best practices. Additionally, quantifiable KPIs provide clear insights into performance trends and areas for improvement, facilitating data-driven decision-making and continuous improvement efforts.

To ensure measurability and quantifiability of KPIs, organizations may use the following CLI commands or techniques:

Define measurement criteria:
shellCopy code

```
$ echo "Define measurement criteria for Service Desk
KPIs."
```

rubyCopy code

```
$ vi measurement_criteria.txt
Select quantitative metrics:
```

perlCopy code

```
$    grep    -i    "quantitative    metrics"
service_desk_kpi_selection_criteria.txt
```

shellCopy code

```
$ curl -X GET http://quantitative_metrics_registry.com
Establish data collection mechanisms:
```

cssCopy code

```
$    ansible-playbook    -i    inventory_file
data_collection_playbook.yml
```

The third selection criterion for Service Desk KPIs is actionability and relevance to decision-making. KPIs should provide actionable insights that enable organizations to identify areas for improvement and take corrective actions to enhance service desk performance. Actionable KPIs should highlight specific issues, trends, or patterns that require attention and intervention to drive meaningful change and improvement. Additionally, KPIs should be relevant to decision-making processes, helping organizations prioritize initiatives, allocate resources, and implement strategies to optimize service desk operations.

To ensure actionability and relevance to decision-making, organizations may use the following CLI commands or techniques:

Define action plans for KPIs:

shellCopy code

$ echo "Develop action plans for addressing performance issues identified by Service Desk KPIs."

rubyCopy code

```
$ vi service_desk_kpi_action_plans.txt
```

Establish escalation procedures:

perlCopy code

```
$ grep -i "escalation procedures" service_desk_kpi_selection_criteria.txt
```

shellCopy code

```
$ curl -X GET http://escalation_procedures_registry.com
```

Implement continuous improvement processes:

cssCopy code

```
$ ansible-playbook -i inventory_file continuous_improvement_playbook.yml
```

The fourth selection criterion for Service Desk KPIs is measurability and consistency over time. KPIs should be consistently measurable and comparable over time to track trends, assess progress, and evaluate the impact of improvement initiatives. Consistent KPIs enable organizations to identify patterns and anomalies in performance, detect underlying issues or root causes, and monitor the effectiveness of interventions and changes implemented to address performance gaps.

To ensure measurability and consistency over time, organizations may use the following CLI commands or techniques:

Establish baseline measurements:

perlCopy code

```
$ grep -i "baseline measurements" service_desk_kpi_selection_criteria.txt
```

shellCopy code

```
$ curl -X GET http://baseline_measurements_registry.com
```
Implement regular data collection and reporting:

cssCopy code
```
$          ansible-playbook          -i          inventory_file
regular_reporting_playbook.yml
```
Conduct periodic performance reviews:

shellCopy code
```
$ echo "Conduct periodic reviews of Service Desk KPIs to
assess progress and identify trends."
```
rubyCopy code
```
$ vi service_desk_kpi_review_process.txt
```
By applying these selection criteria, organizations can ensure that their Service Desk KPIs are relevant, measurable, actionable, and consistent over time, enabling them to effectively monitor, manage, and optimize service desk performance to meet customer needs and achieve business objectives.

Examples of common Service Desk Key Performance Indicators (KPIs) encompass a diverse range of metrics used to evaluate the performance and effectiveness of service desk operations. These KPIs provide organizations with valuable insights into various aspects of service desk performance, including responsiveness, efficiency, customer satisfaction, and adherence to service level agreements (SLAs). By tracking and monitoring these KPIs, organizations can identify areas for improvement, drive continuous improvement initiatives, and deliver exceptional customer service. Some examples of common Service Desk KPIs include:

First Call Resolution (FCR) Rate: FCR rate measures the percentage of incidents or service requests resolved on the first contact with the service desk. A high FCR rate indicates efficient problem resolution and minimizes customer inconvenience. To calculate FCR rate, organizations can use the following CLI command:

perlCopy code

```
$ grep -i "first call resolution" service_desk_performance_logs.txt
```

Average Response Time: Average response time measures the average time taken by the service desk to respond to incidents or service requests from the time they are reported. A low average response time indicates prompt service desk responsiveness and customer support. To calculate average response time, organizations can use the following CLI command:

rubyCopy code

```
$ awk '{sum += $1} END {print "Average response time:", sum/NR}' response_time_data.txt
```

Customer Satisfaction Score (CSAT): CSAT measures customer satisfaction levels with the service desk's performance and responsiveness. Customers are typically asked to rate their satisfaction on a scale after interacting with the service desk. A high CSAT score indicates positive customer experiences and satisfaction with the service provided. To collect and analyze CSAT data, organizations can use the following CLI command:

shellCopy code

```
$ curl -X GET http://customer_satisfaction_survey.com
```

Incident Resolution Time: Incident resolution time measures the average time taken by the service desk to resolve incidents or service requests from the time they are reported. A low incident resolution time indicates efficient problem resolution and minimizes downtime for users. To calculate incident resolution time, organizations can use the following CLI command:

rubyCopy code

```
$ awk '{sum += $1} END {print "Average incident resolution time:", sum/NR}' incident_resolution_time_data.txt
```

Service Level Agreement (SLA) Compliance: SLA compliance measures the extent to which the service desk meets the agreed-upon service levels and response times defined in SLAs. SLA compliance is typically expressed as a percentage, with higher percentages indicating better adherence to SLAs. To track SLA compliance, organizations can use the following CLI command:

perlCopy code

```
$ grep -i "SLA breach" service_desk_performance_logs.txt
```

Ticket Volume: Ticket volume measures the total number of incidents or service requests handled by the service desk within a specific period. Monitoring ticket volume helps organizations understand workload trends, allocate resources effectively, and identify peak periods of activity. To analyze ticket volume, organizations can use the following CLI command:

shellCopy code

```
$ wc -l service_desk_tickets.txt
```

Average Handle Time (AHT): AHT measures the average time taken by the service desk to handle each incident or service request, including time spent on diagnosis, troubleshooting, and resolution. A low AHT indicates efficient service desk operations and streamlined processes. To calculate AHT, organizations can use the following CLI command:

rubyCopy code

```
$ awk '{sum += $1} END {print "Average handle time:",
sum/NR}' handle_time_data.txt
```

Escalation Rate: Escalation rate measures the percentage of incidents or service requests that are escalated to higher support tiers or management for resolution. A high escalation rate may indicate inefficiencies in problem resolution processes or the need for additional training and resources. To calculate escalation rate, organizations can use the following CLI command:

perlCopy code

```
$      grep      -i      "incident      escalation"
service_desk_performance_logs.txt
```

Self-Service Adoption Rate: Self-service adoption rate measures the percentage of incidents or service requests that are resolved through self-service channels, such as knowledge bases or automated systems, without the need for human intervention. A high self-service adoption rate indicates successful implementation and utilization of self-service options. To track self-service adoption rate, organizations can use the following CLI command:

perlCopy code

```
$           grep           -i           "self-service"
service_desk_performance_logs.txt
```

Agent Utilization Rate: Agent utilization rate measures the percentage of time that service desk agents spend actively engaged in resolving incidents or service requests, compared to their total available working hours. A high agent utilization rate indicates efficient resource utilization and workload management. To calculate agent utilization rate, organizations can use the following CLI command:

rubyCopy code

```
$ awk '{sum += $1} END {print "Agent utilization rate:", sum/NR}' agent_utilization_data.txt
```

These examples illustrate the diverse range of Service Desk KPIs that organizations can track to monitor performance, identify improvement opportunities, and deliver exceptional customer service. By selecting and monitoring relevant KPIs, organizations can optimize service desk operations, improve customer satisfaction, and achieve business objectives effectively.

Chapter 3: Setting SMART Goals for Service Desk Optimization

The components of SMART goals provide a framework for setting objectives that are Specific, Measurable, Achievable, Relevant, and Time-bound. This framework ensures that goals are well-defined, actionable, and aligned with organizational priorities, facilitating effective planning, execution, and evaluation of performance. SMART goals help individuals and organizations clarify their objectives, establish clear criteria for success, and track progress towards achieving desired outcomes. Each component of SMART goals plays a crucial role in ensuring goal clarity, feasibility, and effectiveness.

Specific: The first component of SMART goals is specificity, which involves clearly defining the desired outcome or objective. Specific goals provide clarity and focus, helping individuals understand what needs to be accomplished and why it is important. To ensure specificity, goals should answer the questions: What do I want to achieve? Who is involved? Where will it happen? When will it be accomplished? Why is it important? For example, a specific goal could be "Increase customer satisfaction ratings by 10% within the next six months."

Measurable: The second component of SMART goals is measurability, which involves defining criteria for evaluating progress and success. Measurable goals enable individuals to track their performance and determine whether they are making progress towards achieving the desired outcome. To ensure measurability, goals should include specific metrics, targets, or milestones that can be quantified and monitored over time. For example, a measurable goal could be "Achieve a customer satisfaction rating of 90% or higher on quarterly surveys."

Achievable: The third component of SMART goals is achievability, which involves setting objectives that are realistic and attainable given available resources, capabilities, and constraints. Achievable goals challenge individuals to stretch beyond their current abilities but are within reach with effort and commitment. To ensure achievability, goals should consider factors such as time, resources, skills, and external dependencies. For example, an achievable goal could be "Implement a new customer feedback system within six months with the existing IT budget and staffing resources."

Relevant: The fourth component of SMART goals is relevance, which involves ensuring that objectives are aligned with broader organizational goals, priorities, and strategic objectives. Relevant goals contribute to the overall mission and vision of the organization, driving progress and value creation. To ensure relevance, goals should be directly linked to key business priorities and address pressing challenges or opportunities. For example, a relevant goal could be "Improve customer satisfaction ratings to support the organization's goal of becoming the market leader in customer service excellence."

Time-bound: The fifth component of SMART goals is time-bound, which involves setting a specific timeframe or deadline for achieving the objective. Time-bound goals create a sense of urgency, accountability, and focus, helping individuals prioritize tasks and allocate resources effectively. To ensure time-boundness, goals should have clear start and end dates, as well as interim milestones or deadlines for tracking progress. For example, a time-bound goal could be "Launch the new customer feedback system by the end of the third quarter to coincide with the peak customer engagement period."

In summary, the components of SMART goals—Specific, Measurable, Achievable, Relevant, and Time-bound—provide a structured approach to goal setting that enhances clarity, accountability, and effectiveness. By incorporating each component into goal-setting processes, individuals and organizations can establish objectives that are well-defined, actionable, and aligned with strategic priorities, driving success and continuous improvement.

The goal-setting process for service desk improvement is a systematic approach to defining objectives, identifying areas for enhancement, and establishing actionable targets to enhance the performance and effectiveness of service desk operations. This process involves several key steps aimed at clarifying objectives, aligning goals with organizational priorities, and implementing strategies to achieve desired outcomes. By following a structured goal-setting process, service desk managers can enhance service delivery, optimize workflows, and improve customer satisfaction levels.

Assessment of Current State: The first step in the goal-setting process for service desk improvement is to assess the current state of service desk operations. This involves conducting a comprehensive evaluation of existing processes, performance metrics, and customer feedback to identify strengths, weaknesses, and areas for improvement. Service desk managers can use various techniques, such as performance analysis tools and customer surveys, to gather data and insights about service desk performance. For example, they may use the grep command to search through service desk logs for patterns or trends related to incident resolution times or customer satisfaction scores.

cssCopy code

```
$ grep -i "incident resolution time" service_desk_logs.txt
```

Defining Improvement Objectives: Based on the assessment of the current state, service desk managers can then define improvement objectives that address identified areas for enhancement. These objectives should be specific, measurable, achievable, relevant, and time-bound (SMART) to ensure clarity and effectiveness. For example, an improvement objective could be to reduce average response times for incoming service requests by 20% within the next six months. To define SMART objectives, service desk managers may use techniques such as brainstorming sessions or workshops to gather input from key stakeholders and team members.

shellCopy code

```
$ echo "Define SMART improvement objectives for service desk operations."
```

Identifying Key Performance Indicators (KPIs): Once improvement objectives are defined, service desk managers need to identify key performance indicators (KPIs) that will be used to measure progress towards achieving these objectives. KPIs should be aligned with improvement objectives and reflect critical aspects of service desk performance, such as response times, first call resolution rates, and customer satisfaction scores.

Service desk managers can use a combination of quantitative data analysis and stakeholder input to select relevant KPIs. For example, they may use the awk command to calculate average response times from historical data.

rubyCopy code

```
$ awk '{sum += $1} END {print "Average response time:", sum/NR}' response_time_data.txt
```

Establishing Action Plans: With improvement objectives and KPIs in place, service desk managers can then develop action plans outlining specific strategies and initiatives to achieve the defined goals. Action plans should include detailed steps, responsibilities, timelines, and resource requirements to ensure clarity and accountability. Service desk managers may use project management tools or collaboration platforms to document and track action plans. For example, they may use the vi editor to create a detailed action plan document.

rubyCopy code

```
$ vi action_plan.txt
```

Monitoring and Reviewing Progress: Once action plans are implemented, service desk managers need to continuously monitor and review progress towards achieving improvement objectives. This involves regularly tracking performance against established KPIs, identifying any deviations or obstacles, and making adjustments to action plans as needed. Service desk managers can use data visualization tools or dashboard software to monitor KPIs in real-time and generate performance reports. For example, they may use the curl command to retrieve data from a KPI tracking dashboard.

shellCopy code

```
$ curl -X GET http://kpi_dashboard.com
```

Iterative Improvement: The goal-setting process for service desk improvement is iterative and ongoing, requiring continuous evaluation, adjustment, and refinement of improvement objectives and action plans. Service desk managers should solicit feedback from stakeholders, analyze performance trends, and identify opportunities for further optimization. By adopting a culture of continuous improvement, service desk managers can drive long-term success and adaptability in service delivery.

Overall, the goal-setting process for service desk improvement involves a structured approach to defining objectives, identifying KPIs, establishing action plans, monitoring progress, and driving iterative improvement. By following this process, service desk managers can enhance the performance, efficiency, and effectiveness of service desk operations, ultimately improving customer satisfaction and driving organizational success.

Chapter 4: Data Collection and Analysis Techniques

Methods for collecting service desk data are essential for gaining insights into the performance, efficiency, and effectiveness of service desk operations. These methods encompass various techniques and tools used to gather, analyze, and interpret data related to incident management, service requests, customer interactions, and other key aspects of service desk activities. By collecting and analyzing relevant data, organizations can identify trends, patterns, and areas for improvement, enabling them to optimize service delivery and enhance customer satisfaction levels. Several methods can be employed to collect service desk data effectively.

Ticketing Systems: Ticketing systems are commonly used tools for collecting and managing data related to incidents, service requests, and other support activities handled by the service desk. These systems allow service desk agents to log, track, and prioritize tickets, capturing essential information such as the nature of the issue, the customer's contact details, and the status of the ticket. Organizations can utilize ticketing systems like JIRA, ServiceNow, or Zendesk to collect comprehensive data on service desk interactions.

rubyCopy code

```
$ sudo apt install jira
```

Customer Surveys: Customer surveys are valuable tools for collecting feedback and satisfaction ratings from users who have interacted with the service desk.

Organizations can design and distribute surveys to gather insights into customer experiences, preferences, and areas for improvement. Survey responses can provide valuable qualitative data that complements quantitative metrics collected through other methods. Organizations may use online survey platforms like SurveyMonkey or Google Forms to create and distribute customer surveys.

shellCopy code

```
$ curl -X GET http://survey_platform.com
```

Call Logging Systems: Call logging systems enable organizations to capture data related to telephone calls and other forms of communication received by the service desk. These systems record details such as the caller's phone number, the nature of the inquiry, and the duration of the call. By analyzing call logs, organizations can identify common issues, peak call times, and opportunities to improve response times and call handling procedures. Call logging systems can be integrated with ticketing systems or deployed as standalone solutions.

perlCopy code

```
$ grep -i "call logging" service_desk_logs.txt
```

Performance Metrics: Performance metrics such as first call resolution rate, average response time, and incident resolution time provide quantitative data on service desk performance and efficiency. Organizations can collect and analyze these metrics using reporting tools or dashboard software, enabling them to track trends, identify bottlenecks, and measure progress towards performance goals. Performance metrics are typically derived from data stored in ticketing systems or call logging systems.

rubyCopy code

```
$ awk '{sum += $1} END {print "Average response time:", sum/NR}' response_time_data.txt
```

Incident and Problem Records: Incident and problem records contain detailed information about specific incidents, problems, and their resolutions. By analyzing incident and problem records, organizations can identify recurring issues, root causes, and opportunities for preventive action. Incident and problem records are typically stored in ticketing systems or incident management databases, where they can be accessed and analyzed by service desk managers and analysts.

perlCopy code

```
$ grep -i "incident record" incident_records_database.txt
```

Feedback Channels: Feedback channels such as email, chat, or social media provide additional avenues for collecting data and insights from customers and end-users. Organizations can encourage users to provide feedback or report issues through these channels, allowing them to capture real-time feedback and address concerns promptly. Feedback channels can supplement data collected through other methods, providing a comprehensive view of customer sentiment and satisfaction levels.

shellCopy code

```
$ tail -n 1000 feedback_emails.txt
```

Automation and Monitoring Tools: Automation and monitoring tools enable organizations to collect real-time data on system performance, availability, and health. These tools can capture metrics such as server uptime, network latency, and application performance, which may impact service desk operations and customer experience. By monitoring key performance indicators (KPIs) using automation tools like Nagios or Prometheus, organizations can proactively detect and resolve issues before they escalate.

luaCopy code

```
$ systemctl status nagios
```

Knowledge Base Usage: Knowledge base usage data provides insights into the effectiveness and relevance of self-service resources available to users. Organizations can track metrics such as the number of knowledge base searches, article views, and user feedback to assess the usefulness of knowledge base content and identify areas for improvement. Knowledge base usage data can inform content creation and maintenance efforts, ensuring that self-service resources meet users' needs effectively.

perlCopy code

```
$ grep -i "knowledge base usage" knowledge_base_logs.txt
```

By leveraging these methods for collecting service desk data, organizations can gain valuable insights into service desk performance, customer satisfaction levels, and areas for improvement. By analyzing and interpreting data collected through these methods, organizations can make informed decisions, implement targeted improvements, and enhance the overall effectiveness and efficiency of their service desk operations.

Analytical tools and techniques play a crucial role in evaluating Key Performance Indicators (KPIs) to gain valuable insights into organizational performance, identify trends, and make data-driven decisions. These tools enable organizations to analyze KPI data effectively, identify areas for improvement, and track progress towards strategic objectives. By leveraging analytical tools and techniques, organizations can optimize performance, enhance efficiency, and achieve their business goals.

Data Visualization Tools: Data visualization tools such as Tableau, Power BI, and Google Data Studio enable organizations to create visual representations of KPI data, including charts, graphs, and dashboards. These tools allow stakeholders to interpret complex datasets more easily, identify patterns, and trends, and gain actionable insights at a glance. For example, organizations can use Tableau to create interactive dashboards that visualize KPI trends over time and drill down into specific metrics.

```ruby
$ sudo apt install tableau
```

Trend Analysis: Trend analysis involves examining historical KPI data to identify patterns, correlations, and trends over time. By analyzing trends, organizations can assess performance changes, forecast future outcomes, and identify areas for improvement. Trend analysis can be performed using statistical techniques such as linear regression or moving averages to identify underlying patterns and anomalies in KPI data. For example, organizations can use the Excel tool to perform trend analysis on historical KPI data.

rubyCopy code

```
$ excel trend_analysis.xlsx
```

Comparative Analysis: Comparative analysis involves comparing KPI data across different time periods, departments, or benchmarking against industry standards or competitors. By comparing KPI performance, organizations can identify areas of strength and weakness, benchmark performance against peers, and set realistic improvement targets. Comparative analysis can be performed using tools like Microsoft Excel or specialized business intelligence software that support data comparison and benchmarking features.

rubyCopy code

```
$ excel comparative_analysis.xlsx
```

Root Cause Analysis: Root cause analysis (RCA) is a technique used to identify the underlying causes of performance issues or deviations from KPI targets. By conducting RCA, organizations can identify the root causes of problems, rather than just addressing symptoms, and implement targeted solutions to address them. RCA techniques include methods such as fishbone diagrams, 5 Whys analysis, and Pareto analysis. For example, organizations can use the fishbone diagram to visualize potential root causes of performance issues.

```ruby
rubyCopy code
$ draw fishbone_diagram.drawio
```

Correlation Analysis: Correlation analysis involves examining the relationship between different KPIs to identify correlations or dependencies. By analyzing correlations, organizations can uncover relationships between variables, understand how changes in one KPI affect others, and identify opportunities for optimization. Correlation analysis can be performed using statistical techniques such as Pearson correlation coefficient or Spearman rank correlation coefficient. For example, organizations can use Python with libraries like Pandas and NumPy to conduct correlation analysis on KPI datasets.

```ruby
rubyCopy code
$ python correlation_analysis.py
```

Predictive Analytics: Predictive analytics involves using historical KPI data and statistical models to forecast future performance and trends. By leveraging predictive analytics, organizations can anticipate future outcomes, identify potential risks or opportunities, and make proactive decisions to optimize performance. Predictive analytics techniques include time series forecasting, regression analysis, and machine learning algorithms. For example, organizations can use the R programming language with the forecast package to perform time series forecasting on KPI data.

```ruby
rubyCopy code
$ Rscript predictive_analytics.R
```

Text Mining and Sentiment Analysis: Text mining and sentiment analysis techniques involve analyzing unstructured data such as customer feedback, social media comments, and support tickets to extract insights and sentiment trends related to KPIs. By analyzing text data, organizations can understand customer sentiment, identify emerging issues, and prioritize improvement initiatives. Text mining and sentiment analysis can be performed using natural language processing (NLP) techniques and tools like Python with libraries such as NLTK and scikit-learn. For example, organizations can use Python scripts to perform sentiment analysis on customer feedback data.

rubyCopy code

```
$ python sentiment_analysis.py
```

By leveraging these analytical tools and techniques, organizations can effectively evaluate KPIs, gain actionable insights, and drive continuous improvement in performance and efficiency. Whether it's visualizing data with dashboards, analyzing trends, conducting root cause analysis, or leveraging predictive analytics, these tools empower organizations to make informed decisions and achieve their strategic objectives.

Chapter 5: Monitoring and Measuring Service Desk Metrics

Establishing monitoring processes for Key Performance Indicators (KPIs) is essential for organizations to track performance, identify trends, and make informed decisions to achieve their strategic objectives. Monitoring processes involve the systematic collection, analysis, and interpretation of KPI data to assess performance against targets, identify areas for improvement, and drive continuous optimization. By implementing robust monitoring processes, organizations can enhance accountability, transparency, and effectiveness in managing performance metrics.

Define KPIs: The first step in establishing monitoring processes for KPIs is to define the metrics that are most relevant to the organization's goals and objectives. KPIs should be specific, measurable, achievable, relevant, and time-bound (SMART), aligning with the organization's strategic priorities. Organizations may use techniques such as brainstorming sessions or stakeholder consultations to identify and prioritize KPIs that reflect key aspects of performance.

shellCopy code

```
$ echo "Define SMART KPIs aligned with organizational goals."
```

Select Data Sources: Once KPIs are defined, organizations need to identify the data sources that will be used to collect relevant performance data. Data sources may include internal systems such as CRM platforms, ERP systems, or ticketing systems, as well as external sources such as customer surveys or market research reports. Organizations should ensure that data sources are accurate, reliable, and capable of providing timely insights into KPI performance.

perlCopy code

```
$ grep -i "data sources" monitoring_plan.txt
```

Establish Data Collection Mechanisms: With data sources identified, organizations need to establish mechanisms for collecting, storing, and managing KPI data effectively. This may involve implementing data collection tools or systems, setting up automated data feeds, or defining manual data entry processes. Organizations should ensure that data collection mechanisms comply with data privacy regulations and security best practices to protect sensitive information.

rubyCopy code

```
$ sudo apt install data_collection_tool
```

Set Baselines and Targets: Once data collection mechanisms are in place, organizations should establish baseline values and targets for each KPI to provide benchmarks for performance evaluation. Baselines represent current performance levels, while targets define desired performance levels that the organization aims to achieve within a specific timeframe. Baselines and targets should be realistic, achievable, and aligned with organizational goals.

shellCopy code

```
$ echo "Set baseline values and targets for each KPI."
```

Implement Monitoring Tools: To monitor KPI performance effectively, organizations need to implement monitoring tools or software that enable real-time tracking and visualization of KPI data. Monitoring tools may include business intelligence platforms, dashboard software, or custom-built analytics solutions. These tools should provide stakeholders with intuitive interfaces for accessing KPI data, generating reports, and receiving alerts for performance deviations.

rubyCopy code

```ruby
$ sudo apt install monitoring_tool
```

Develop Reporting Mechanisms: In addition to real-time monitoring, organizations should establish reporting mechanisms to communicate KPI performance to relevant stakeholders. Reports may include dashboards, scorecards, or periodic performance reports that highlight key insights, trends, and areas for improvement. Organizations should tailor reporting formats and frequency to the needs of different stakeholders, ensuring that information is presented in a clear and actionable manner.

shellCopy code

```shell
$ echo "Develop reporting mechanisms for communicating KPI performance."
```

Conduct Regular Reviews: To ensure the effectiveness of monitoring processes, organizations should conduct regular reviews of KPI performance data and monitoring procedures. Reviews may involve analyzing trends, identifying performance gaps, and assessing the impact of corrective actions or improvement initiatives. By conducting regular reviews, organizations can identify opportunities for optimization and make adjustments to monitoring processes as needed.

perlCopy code

```
$ grep -i "regular reviews" monitoring_plan.txt
```

Implement Continuous Improvement: Monitoring processes for KPIs should be dynamic and responsive to changing business needs and objectives. Organizations should continuously evaluate and refine monitoring processes based on feedback, performance trends, and emerging best practices. By embracing a culture of continuous improvement, organizations can enhance the effectiveness of monitoring processes and drive better outcomes in performance management.

shellCopy code

```
$ echo "Implement continuous improvement practices for monitoring processes."
```

By following these steps and establishing robust monitoring processes for KPIs, organizations can gain valuable insights into performance, drive accountability, and make data-driven decisions to achieve their strategic objectives effectively. Monitoring processes provide organizations with the visibility and transparency needed to track progress, identify areas for improvement, and drive continuous optimization in performance management. Measuring performance against set benchmarks is a fundamental aspect of performance management, providing organizations with a means to assess progress, identify areas for improvement, and track alignment with strategic objectives. Benchmarks serve as reference points or standards against which performance can be evaluated, enabling organizations to gauge their effectiveness, efficiency, and competitiveness in achieving desired outcomes. By establishing clear benchmarks and implementing robust measurement processes, organizations can enhance accountability, drive continuous improvement, and optimize performance across various domains.

Define Benchmark Metrics: The first step in measuring performance against set benchmarks is to define the metrics or key performance indicators (KPIs) that will serve as benchmarks for evaluation. These benchmark metrics should be relevant, measurable, and aligned with organizational goals and objectives. Organizations may select benchmark metrics based on industry standards, best practices, or internal performance targets, ensuring that they provide meaningful insights into performance.

shellCopy code

```shell
$ echo "Define benchmark metrics aligned with organizational goals."
```

Set Performance Benchmarks: Once benchmark metrics are defined, organizations need to establish performance benchmarks or targets against which actual performance will be compared. Benchmarks should be realistic, achievable, and based on historical performance data, industry benchmarks, or strategic objectives. Organizations may set benchmarks for different time periods, such as monthly, quarterly, or annually, to track progress and evaluate performance over time.

shellCopy code

```
$ echo "Set performance benchmarks for each
benchmark metric."
```

Collect Performance Data: With benchmarks defined, organizations need to collect relevant performance data to assess actual performance against set benchmarks. This may involve gathering data from various sources, such as internal systems, customer surveys, or market research reports. Data collection processes should be standardized, consistent, and comply with data privacy regulations to ensure the accuracy and integrity of performance data.

perlCopy code

```
$ grep -i "performance data"
data_collection_process.txt
```

Analyze Performance Data: Once performance data is collected, organizations need to analyze the data to assess actual performance against set benchmarks. This may involve conducting statistical analysis, trend analysis, or comparative analysis to identify performance trends, deviations, and outliers. Organizations may use tools such as Microsoft Excel, Tableau, or Python for data analysis, generating insights into performance drivers and areas for improvement.

rubyCopy code

```
$ python performance_analysis.py
```

Compare Actual Performance to Benchmarks: After analyzing performance data, organizations need to compare actual performance metrics to set benchmarks to determine whether performance targets have been met, exceeded, or fallen short. This comparison enables organizations to identify performance gaps and take corrective action to address areas of underperformance. Organizations may use formulas or calculations to compare actual performance to benchmarks, calculating variance or deviation from targets.

swiftCopy code

```
$ awk '{print "Actual performance - Benchmark =", $1
- $2}' performance_comparison.txt
```

Identify Performance Discrepancies: In comparing actual performance to benchmarks, organizations should identify any discrepancies or deviations from set targets. Performance discrepancies may indicate areas of strength or weakness, highlighting opportunities for improvement or optimization. By identifying performance discrepancies, organizations can prioritize resources and initiatives to address critical areas and drive performance improvement.

perlCopy code

```
$ grep -i "performance discrepancies"
performance_analysis_report.txt
```

Implement Performance Improvement Strategies: Based on the analysis of performance data and identification of discrepancies, organizations should develop and implement performance improvement strategies to address areas of underperformance and optimize performance. These strategies may include process optimization, resource reallocation, skills development, or technology adoption to enhance efficiency and effectiveness. Organizations should monitor the implementation of improvement strategies and track their impact on performance metrics over time.

shellCopy code

```
$ echo "Implement performance improvement strategies to address performance gaps."
```

Monitor Progress and Adjust Benchmarks: Performance measurement is an iterative process, and organizations should continuously monitor progress against benchmarks and adjust benchmarks as needed to reflect changing business conditions, market dynamics, or strategic priorities. By regularly reviewing performance metrics and benchmarks, organizations can ensure alignment with evolving goals and objectives, driving continuous improvement and adaptation to changing circumstances.

perlCopy code

```
$ grep -i "monitor progress" performance_management_plan.txt
```

By following these steps and measuring performance against set benchmarks, organizations can gain valuable insights into their performance, identify opportunities for improvement, and drive continuous optimization across various domains. Benchmarks provide organizations with a means to assess performance objectively, establish accountability, and track progress towards strategic objectives effectively. Through regular monitoring, analysis, and adjustment of benchmarks, organizations can optimize performance and achieve sustainable growth and success.

Chapter 6: Continuous Improvement Strategies

Continuous improvement in service desk operations is essential for organizations to adapt to changing customer needs, technological advancements, and business requirements. By embracing a culture of continuous improvement, organizations can enhance service delivery, increase efficiency, and drive customer satisfaction. Continuous improvement involves systematically identifying opportunities for enhancement, implementing changes, and measuring the impact of those changes to ensure ongoing optimization of service desk operations. Through continuous improvement initiatives, organizations can stay competitive, agile, and responsive in the dynamic business environment.

Identify Improvement Opportunities: The first step in continuous improvement is to identify areas within service desk operations that could benefit from enhancement. This may involve analyzing customer feedback, monitoring service desk metrics, or conducting root cause analysis of recurring issues. By soliciting input from stakeholders and frontline staff, organizations can gain valuable insights into pain points, inefficiencies, and areas for optimization within service desk operations.

perlCopy code

```
$ grep -i "improvement opportunities" feedback_analysis.txt
```

Prioritize Improvement Initiatives: Once improvement opportunities are identified, organizations need to prioritize initiatives based on their potential impact and feasibility. Prioritization may involve assessing the urgency of the issue, the resources required for implementation, and the alignment with strategic objectives. By prioritizing improvement initiatives, organizations can focus their efforts on areas that offer the greatest potential for enhancing service desk operations and delivering value to customers.

shellCopy code

```
$ echo "Prioritize improvement initiatives based on potential impact and feasibility."
```

Develop Improvement Plans: With improvement initiatives prioritized, organizations should develop detailed improvement plans outlining the objectives, actions, timelines, and responsibilities for each initiative. Improvement plans should be SMART (Specific, Measurable, Achievable, Relevant, Time-bound) and clearly communicate the desired outcomes and steps for implementation. By developing structured improvement plans, organizations can ensure accountability, alignment, and effective execution of improvement initiatives.

rubyCopy code

```
$ vim improvement_plan.txt
```

Implement Changes: Once improvement plans are developed, organizations need to implement changes within service desk operations according to the defined action steps and timelines. Implementation may involve updating processes, procedures, or technology systems, as well as providing training and support to staff. Organizations should communicate changes effectively to stakeholders and solicit feedback throughout the implementation process to ensure smooth transition and adoption.

rubyCopy code

```ruby
$ git commit -m "Implement changes according to improvement plan."
```

Monitor Performance: Following the implementation of changes, organizations should monitor performance metrics and key performance indicators (KPIs) to assess the impact of improvement initiatives on service desk operations. Monitoring may involve tracking metrics such as first call resolution rate, average response time, or customer satisfaction scores to gauge the effectiveness of changes. Organizations should establish regular reporting mechanisms and review performance data to identify trends, successes, and areas for further improvement.

shellCopy code

```shell
$ tail -n 100 performance_metrics.log
```

Gather Feedback: In addition to monitoring performance metrics, organizations should actively seek feedback from stakeholders, including customers, frontline staff, and management, regarding the impact of improvement initiatives on service desk operations. Feedback may be collected through surveys, focus groups, or one-on-one discussions to gather insights into the effectiveness of changes and identify any unintended consequences or areas requiring adjustment.

cssCopy code

```
$ survey_tool --collect feedback
```

Analyze Results: Once feedback is gathered, organizations should analyze the results to assess the overall effectiveness of improvement initiatives and identify areas for refinement or further enhancement. Analysis may involve comparing performance data before and after the implementation of changes, conducting root cause analysis of any issues or challenges, and identifying best practices or lessons learned for future improvement efforts.

rubyCopy code

```
$ python feedback_analysis.py
```

Iterate and Adapt: Continuous improvement is an iterative process, and organizations should continuously iterate, adapt, and refine service desk operations based on feedback, performance data, and changing business needs. This may involve revisiting improvement plans, prioritizing new initiatives, or adjusting processes and procedures to address evolving requirements. By embracing a cycle of continuous improvement, organizations can drive ongoing optimization, innovation, and excellence in service desk operations.

shellCopy code

```
$ echo "Iterate and adapt service desk operations based on feedback and performance data."
```

By prioritizing continuous improvement in service desk operations and following structured processes for identifying, prioritizing, implementing, and evaluating improvement initiatives, organizations can enhance service quality, increase efficiency, and drive customer satisfaction. Continuous improvement fosters a culture of innovation, collaboration, and accountability, enabling organizations to adapt to change, seize opportunities, and achieve sustainable success in today's competitive landscape.

Strategies for iterative enhancement of service desk performance play a crucial role in ensuring continuous improvement and optimization of service delivery processes. Iterative enhancement involves a cyclical approach to identifying, implementing, and evaluating improvements in service desk operations to meet evolving customer needs and business objectives. By embracing iterative enhancement strategies, organizations can drive efficiency, agility, and customer satisfaction within their service desk operations, ultimately leading to enhanced performance and competitive advantage in the market.

Establish Continuous Feedback Loops: One of the key strategies for iterative enhancement is to establish continuous feedback loops within service desk operations. Feedback loops enable organizations to gather insights from various stakeholders, including customers, frontline staff, and management, regarding their experiences and perceptions of service delivery. By soliciting feedback through channels such as surveys, focus groups, or incident reports, organizations can identify areas for improvement and prioritize enhancement initiatives based on real-time input.

shellCopy code

```
$ echo "Establish continuous feedback loops to gather
insights from stakeholders."
```
Analyze Performance Data: In addition to gathering feedback, organizations should analyze performance data to identify trends, patterns, and areas of opportunity within service desk operations. Performance data may include key performance indicators (KPIs) such as response times, resolution rates, and customer satisfaction scores, which provide insights into the effectiveness and efficiency of service delivery. By leveraging data analysis techniques such as statistical analysis or trend analysis, organizations can pinpoint areas for iterative enhancement and track the impact of improvement initiatives over time.

perlCopy code

```
$      grep      -i      "performance      data"
performance_analysis_report.txt
```

Prioritize Improvement Initiatives: Once feedback is gathered and performance data is analyzed, organizations need to prioritize improvement initiatives based on their potential impact and feasibility. Prioritization may involve assessing the urgency of issues, the resources required for implementation, and the alignment with strategic objectives. By prioritizing enhancement initiatives, organizations can focus their efforts on initiatives that offer the greatest potential for driving meaningful improvements in service desk performance.

shellCopy code

```
$ echo "Prioritize improvement initiatives based on
potential impact and feasibility."
```

Implement Quick Wins: In addition to prioritizing long-term improvement initiatives, organizations should identify and implement quick wins – small, low-cost enhancements that can be implemented rapidly to deliver immediate benefits. Quick wins help build momentum for continuous improvement efforts and demonstrate tangible progress to stakeholders. Examples of quick wins may include streamlining processes, providing additional training to staff, or implementing minor system enhancements to address common pain points.

rubyCopy code

```
$ git commit -m "Implement quick wins to deliver immediate benefits."
```

Conduct Pilot Projects: To test the feasibility and effectiveness of larger-scale improvement initiatives, organizations may conduct pilot projects in controlled environments before full-scale implementation. Pilot projects enable organizations to evaluate the impact of proposed changes on service desk performance, gather feedback from stakeholders, and identify any unforeseen challenges or issues that need to be addressed. By conducting pilot projects, organizations can minimize risks and optimize the success of improvement initiatives.

rubyCopy code

```
$ docker-compose up -d pilot_project_environment
```

Monitor and Measure Impact: Throughout the iterative enhancement process, organizations should continuously monitor and measure the impact of improvement initiatives on service desk performance.

This may involve tracking key performance indicators (KPIs) before and after the implementation of changes, conducting surveys to gauge customer satisfaction, or soliciting feedback from frontline staff regarding their experiences. By monitoring performance metrics and gathering feedback, organizations can assess the effectiveness of improvement initiatives and make data-driven decisions to optimize service desk operations.

shellCopy code

```
$ tail -n 100 performance_metrics.log
```

Iterate Based on Feedback: Based on the results of performance monitoring and feedback gathering, organizations should iterate and refine their enhancement strategies to address any identified gaps or opportunities for improvement. Iteration may involve adjusting processes, procedures, or technology solutions based on stakeholder input and performance data. By embracing a cycle of continuous iteration, organizations can adapt to changing circumstances, refine their approaches, and drive ongoing improvement in service desk performance.

shellCopy code

```
$ echo "Iterate and refine enhancement strategies based on feedback and performance data."
```

Foster a Culture of Continuous Improvement: Ultimately, the success of iterative enhancement strategies depends on fostering a culture of continuous improvement within the organization. This involves empowering employees to contribute ideas, experiment with new approaches, and embrace change as a catalyst for growth and innovation. By promoting a culture of

continuous improvement, organizations can harness the collective intelligence and creativity of their workforce to drive sustained excellence in service desk operations.
shellCopy code

```
$ echo "Foster a culture of continuous improvement to drive sustained excellence."
```

By embracing strategies for iterative enhancement of service desk performance, organizations can continuously adapt and evolve their service delivery processes to meet the evolving needs and expectations of customers. Through continuous feedback, data-driven decision-making, and a commitment to ongoing improvement, organizations can drive efficiency, effectiveness, and customer satisfaction within their service desk operations, ultimately contributing to their long-term success and competitiveness in the market.

Chapter 7: Implementing Performance Dashboards and Reporting

Designing effective performance dashboards is essential for organizations to gain insights into their operations, monitor key performance indicators (KPIs), and make informed decisions to drive improvement. A well-designed performance dashboard provides stakeholders with a visual representation of critical metrics and trends, allowing them to quickly assess performance, identify areas of concern, and take corrective action when necessary. In designing effective performance dashboards, organizations should consider factors such as audience needs, data visualization best practices, and dashboard interactivity to ensure usability and effectiveness in supporting decision-making processes.

Define Dashboard Objectives: The first step in designing an effective performance dashboard is to define its objectives and purpose. Organizations should identify the specific goals they aim to achieve with the dashboard, such as tracking service desk performance, monitoring customer satisfaction, or analyzing incident trends. By clearly defining objectives, organizations can ensure that the dashboard provides relevant and actionable insights to its intended audience.

shellCopy code

```
$ echo "Define objectives and purpose of the performance dashboard."
```

Identify Key Metrics: Once objectives are defined, organizations need to identify the key metrics or KPIs that will be displayed on the dashboard to measure performance against strategic goals. Key metrics may include metrics related to service desk efficiency, customer satisfaction scores, incident resolution times, or adherence to service level agreements (SLAs). It is essential to select metrics that are meaningful, measurable, and aligned with organizational objectives.

perlCopy code

```
$     grep    -i    "key    metrics"
performance_dashboard_requirements.txt
```

Choose Data Visualization Techniques: With key metrics identified, organizations should choose appropriate data visualization techniques to represent the data effectively on the dashboard. Data visualization techniques may include charts, graphs, tables, or heatmaps, depending on the nature of the data and the insights stakeholders seek to gain. Organizations should consider factors such as clarity, simplicity, and relevance when selecting visualization techniques to ensure that information is presented in a digestible and actionable format.

shellCopy code

```
$ echo "Choose appropriate data visualization techniques for key metrics."
```

Design Dashboard Layout: The layout of the dashboard plays a crucial role in its usability and effectiveness. Organizations should design the dashboard layout to prioritize critical information, highlight trends and outliers, and guide users' attention to key insights. It is essential to organize information logically, use whitespace effectively to improve readability, and maintain consistency in design elements across the dashboard to enhance user experience.

```ruby
Copy code
$ vim performance_dashboard_layout_design.txt
```

Ensure Interactivity and Drill-Down Capabilities: To enhance the usability of the dashboard, organizations should incorporate interactivity and drill-down capabilities that allow users to explore data in more detail. Interactive features such as filters, dropdown menus, or clickable elements enable users to customize their view of the data and access additional information as needed. By providing drill-down capabilities, organizations empower users to investigate specific metrics or trends further, facilitating deeper analysis and insight generation.

```shell
Copy code
$ echo "Incorporate interactivity and drill-down capabilities for deeper analysis."
```

Maintain Data Accuracy and Timeliness: An effective performance dashboard relies on accurate and timely data to provide meaningful insights and support decision-making. Organizations should establish processes to ensure the accuracy, completeness, and reliability of data sources feeding into the dashboard. This may involve data validation checks, data cleansing procedures, and regular audits to identify and rectify any discrepancies or anomalies. Additionally, organizations should strive to update the dashboard in real-time or with minimal latency to ensure that stakeholders have access to the most up-to-date information.

```ruby
Copy code
$ cronjob -e
```

Solicit User Feedback and Iteratively Improve: After deploying the performance dashboard, organizations should solicit feedback from users to identify areas for improvement and iteratively enhance the dashboard based on user input. User feedback may reveal usability issues, data visualization preferences, or additional metrics that users find valuable. By incorporating user feedback into the design process, organizations can iteratively improve the dashboard to better meet the needs of its users and drive greater adoption and effectiveness.

cssCopy code

```
$ survey_tool --collect feedback
```

Regularly Review and Update Dashboard: Finally, organizations should establish a process for regularly reviewing and updating the performance dashboard to ensure its continued relevance and effectiveness. This may involve quarterly or biannual reviews to assess dashboard performance, identify emerging trends or shifts in priorities, and make necessary adjustments to metrics, visualization techniques, or layout. By maintaining a proactive approach to dashboard management, organizations can ensure that the dashboard remains a valuable tool for decision-making and performance management.

rubyCopy code

```
$ calendar -e "Dashboard Review"
```

In summary, designing effective performance dashboards requires careful consideration of objectives, key metrics, visualization techniques, layout, interactivity, data accuracy, user feedback, and ongoing maintenance. By following best practices and incorporating stakeholder input throughout the design process, organizations can create dashboards that provide actionable insights, drive informed decision-making, and ultimately contribute to improved performance and organizational success.

Best practices for KPI reporting to stakeholders are essential for ensuring that key performance indicators (KPIs) are effectively communicated, understood, and utilized to drive informed decision-making and organizational performance. KPI reporting serves as a mechanism for providing stakeholders with timely and relevant insights into the performance of critical business processes, enabling them to assess progress towards strategic goals, identify areas for improvement, and make data-driven decisions. By following best practices for KPI reporting, organizations can enhance transparency, accountability, and alignment across the organization, ultimately driving greater success and achievement of strategic objectives.

Define Clear Objectives: The first step in KPI reporting is to define clear objectives for the reporting process. Organizations should identify the specific goals they aim to achieve with KPI reporting, such as improving performance, tracking progress towards strategic objectives, or enhancing accountability. By establishing clear objectives, organizations can ensure that KPI reporting efforts are focused and aligned with broader business priorities.

shellCopy code

```
$ echo "Define clear objectives for KPI reporting."
```

Identify Relevant KPIs: Once objectives are defined, organizations need to identify the most relevant KPIs to report on. Relevant KPIs should be directly linked to organizational goals and strategic priorities, providing stakeholders with insights into the performance of critical business processes. It is essential to select KPIs that are actionable, measurable, and indicative of overall organizational performance.

perlCopy code

```
$ grep -i "relevant KPIs" KPI_selection_criteria.txt
```

Establish Data Sources and Collection Processes: After identifying relevant KPIs, organizations need to establish data sources and collection processes to ensure the accuracy and reliability of KPI data. This may involve integrating data from various systems and sources, implementing data validation checks, and establishing data governance practices to maintain data quality. By ensuring data integrity, organizations can enhance the credibility and trustworthiness of KPI reporting.

shellCopy code

```
$ echo "Establish data sources and collection processes for KPI data."
```

Design Clear and Concise Reports: When designing KPI reports, it is essential to present information in a clear, concise, and easy-to-understand format. Reports should include relevant KPIs, trends over time, and comparisons to targets or benchmarks, enabling stakeholders to quickly assess performance and identify areas of concern. It is also important to use visual aids such as charts, graphs, and tables to enhance readability and comprehension.

rubyCopy code

```
$ vim KPI_report_template.docx
```

Tailor Reports to Audience Needs: KPI reports should be tailored to the specific needs and preferences of different stakeholders. For example, executive-level stakeholders may require high-level summaries and strategic insights, while operational stakeholders may need more detailed information and actionable recommendations. By customizing reports to meet the needs of different audiences, organizations can ensure that stakeholders receive the information they need to make informed decisions.

cssCopy code

```
$ sed -i 's/Executive Summary/Operational Insights/g' KPI_report_template.docx
```

Provide Context and Analysis: In addition to presenting KPI data, reports should provide context and analysis to help stakeholders interpret the information effectively. This may involve explaining trends, identifying root causes of performance issues, and highlighting potential implications for the organization. By providing context and analysis, organizations can ensure that stakeholders have a comprehensive understanding of KPI performance and can make informed decisions based on the information presented.

shellCopy code

```
$ echo "Provide context and analysis to help stakeholders interpret KPI data."
```

Establish Regular Reporting Cadence: To maintain visibility and accountability, organizations should establish a regular reporting cadence for KPI reporting. This may involve monthly, quarterly, or annual reporting cycles, depending on the needs of stakeholders and the frequency of data updates. By establishing a regular reporting cadence, organizations can ensure that stakeholders receive timely and consistent updates on KPI performance and progress towards strategic objectives.

rubyCopy code

```
$ calendar -e "Monthly KPI Reporting"
```

Solicit Feedback and Continuous Improvement: Finally, organizations should solicit feedback from stakeholders on KPI reporting processes and reports and use this feedback to drive continuous improvement. This may involve conducting surveys, holding feedback sessions, or incorporating feedback into the design of future reports. By actively soliciting feedback and continuously improving KPI reporting practices, organizations can enhance the effectiveness and value of KPI reporting to stakeholders.

cssCopy code

```
$ survey_tool --collect feedback
```

In summary, best practices for KPI reporting to stakeholders involve defining clear objectives, identifying relevant KPIs, establishing data sources and collection processes, designing clear and concise reports, tailoring reports to audience needs, providing context and analysis, establishing a regular reporting cadence, and soliciting feedback for continuous improvement. By following these best practices, organizations can enhance transparency, accountability, and alignment across the organization, ultimately driving greater success and achievement of strategic objectives.

Chapter 8: Addressing Challenges in KPI Implementation

Implementing key performance indicators (KPIs) in service desk management can be fraught with challenges, stemming from various factors such as organizational culture, data availability, and stakeholder alignment. Addressing these challenges is crucial for successful KPI implementation and leveraging KPIs effectively to drive performance improvement and operational excellence within the service desk. By understanding and proactively mitigating common challenges, organizations can enhance the likelihood of KPI implementation success and maximize the value derived from performance measurement initiatives.

Lack of Clear Objectives: One of the primary challenges in implementing KPIs in service desk management is the lack of clear objectives or alignment with organizational goals. Without clearly defined objectives, organizations may struggle to identify relevant KPIs or establish meaningful performance targets, leading to confusion and ineffectiveness in performance measurement efforts. To address this challenge, organizations should first establish clear objectives for KPI implementation, ensuring alignment with broader organizational goals and strategic priorities.

shellCopy code

```
$ echo "Establish clear objectives for KPI implementation in service desk management."
```

Data Quality and Availability Issues: Another common challenge in KPI implementation is the quality and availability of data required for performance measurement. Organizations may encounter issues such as incomplete or inaccurate data, disparate data sources, or data silos that hinder their ability to measure and monitor performance effectively. To overcome this challenge, organizations should invest in data quality management practices, including data validation, cleansing, and integration, to ensure that KPI data is accurate, reliable, and readily accessible for analysis.

perlCopy code

```
$ grep -i "data quality" data_quality_management_plan.txt
```

Resistance to Change: Resistance to change among stakeholders, including service desk staff, management, and other relevant parties, can pose a significant challenge to KPI implementation efforts. Resistance may stem from fear of accountability, perceived threats to job roles or autonomy, or skepticism about the value of performance measurement initiatives. To address resistance to change, organizations should foster a culture of transparency, communication, and collaboration, involving stakeholders in the KPI design process and highlighting the benefits of performance measurement for driving improvement and achieving organizational objectives.

cssCopy code

```
$ echo "Foster a culture of transparency and collaboration to address resistance to change."
```

Lack of Stakeholder Buy-In: Related to resistance to change is the challenge of securing stakeholder buy-in for

KPI implementation. Without buy-in from key stakeholders, including senior leadership, frontline staff, and other relevant parties, KPI initiatives may struggle to gain traction and support within the organization. To overcome this challenge, organizations should engage stakeholders early and often, communicating the rationale for KPI implementation, soliciting feedback, and demonstrating the value of performance measurement in driving organizational success.

```css
cssCopy code
$ survey_tool --collect feedback
```

Inadequate Technology Infrastructure: Inadequate technology infrastructure, including outdated or incompatible systems, limited analytics capabilities, or lack of integration between systems, can hinder KPI implementation efforts. Organizations may struggle to collect, analyze, and report on KPI data effectively due to technological constraints. To address this challenge, organizations should invest in modern technology solutions, including service desk management software, analytics platforms, and integration tools, to support KPI implementation and enable data-driven decision-making.

```ruby
rubyCopy code
$ upgrade_technology_infrastructure
```

Difficulty in Defining and Measuring KPIs: Defining and measuring meaningful KPIs that accurately reflect service desk performance can be a complex and challenging process. Organizations may struggle to identify KPIs that are relevant, actionable, and aligned with organizational objectives, leading to ambiguity and inconsistency in performance measurement. To mitigate this challenge, organizations should involve key stakeholders in the KPI definition process, leveraging their expertise and insights to identify KPIs that are meaningful and reflective of service desk performance.

perlCopy code

```
$ grep -i "define KPIs" KPI_definition_workshop_minutes.txt
```

Lack of Continuous Improvement: Finally, a common challenge in KPI implementation is the lack of a culture of continuous improvement, where organizations fail to use KPI data effectively to drive performance improvement initiatives. Without a commitment to ongoing monitoring, analysis, and action based on KPI insights, organizations may struggle to realize the full potential of performance measurement efforts. To address this challenge, organizations should establish processes for regular review and evaluation of KPI performance, identifying opportunities for improvement and taking proactive steps to address performance gaps.

rubyCopy code

```
$ calendar -e "Monthly KPI Performance Review"
```

In summary, common challenges in implementing KPIs in service desk management include lack of clear objectives, data quality and availability issues, resistance to change, lack of stakeholder buy-in, inadequate technology infrastructure, difficulty in defining and measuring KPIs, and lack of a culture of continuous improvement. By addressing these challenges through proactive measures such as clear objective setting, data quality management, stakeholder engagement, technology investment, and fostering a culture of continuous improvement, organizations can enhance the success of KPI implementation initiatives and drive performance improvement within the service desk.

Implementing new processes, systems, or initiatives often comes with its own set of challenges and hurdles that organizations must overcome to achieve success. These implementation hurdles can range from resistance to change among stakeholders to technological constraints and resource limitations. However, by employing effective strategies and approaches, organizations can navigate these hurdles and ensure the successful implementation of their initiatives. Strategies for overcoming implementation hurdles involve proactive planning, effective communication, stakeholder engagement, and continuous improvement efforts to address challenges as they arise and drive successful outcomes.

Proactive Planning and Preparation: A key strategy for overcoming implementation hurdles is proactive planning and preparation. Before embarking on any implementation initiative, organizations should conduct thorough planning, including defining clear objectives, identifying potential challenges and risks, and developing a detailed implementation plan. By anticipating potential hurdles and developing mitigation strategies in advance, organizations can minimize disruptions and ensure a smoother implementation process.

shellCopy code

```
$ echo "Conduct thorough planning and risk assessment before implementation."
```

Stakeholder Engagement and Buy-In: Engaging stakeholders early and securing their buy-in is essential for overcoming implementation hurdles. Stakeholders, including senior leadership, frontline staff, and other relevant parties, should be involved in the planning and decision-making process from the outset. By soliciting input, addressing concerns, and communicating the benefits of the initiative, organizations can build support and commitment among stakeholders, mitigating resistance to change and facilitating a smoother implementation process.

rubyCopy code

```
$ stakeholder_engagement_plan -e "Engage stakeholders in planning and decision-making."
```

Effective Communication: Effective communication is critical for overcoming implementation hurdles and ensuring that stakeholders are informed and aligned throughout the process. Organizations should establish clear channels of communication, providing regular updates, addressing questions and concerns, and soliciting feedback from stakeholders. By fostering open and transparent communication, organizations can build trust, manage expectations, and mitigate misunderstandings that may arise during the implementation process.

shellCopy code

```
$ echo "Establish clear channels of communication and provide regular updates."
```

Training and Development: Providing training and development opportunities for staff is essential for overcoming implementation hurdles related to skill gaps or resistance to new processes or technologies. Organizations should invest in training programs to ensure that staff have the necessary knowledge and skills to adapt to changes effectively. By empowering staff with the tools and resources they need to succeed, organizations can minimize disruption and accelerate the adoption of new initiatives.

cssCopy code

```
$ training_program --deploy
```

Flexibility and Adaptability: Flexibility and adaptability are key attributes for overcoming implementation hurdles, as unforeseen challenges and obstacles may arise during the implementation process. Organizations should be prepared to adjust their plans and strategies as needed, responding to changing circumstances and feedback from stakeholders. By remaining flexible and adaptive, organizations can navigate challenges more effectively and increase the likelihood of successful implementation.

shellCopy code

```
$ echo "Remain flexible and adapt plans as needed based on feedback and changing circumstances."
```

Resource Allocation and Management: Adequate resource allocation and management are essential for overcoming implementation hurdles related to resource constraints or competing priorities. Organizations should carefully allocate resources, including personnel, budget, and time, to support the implementation initiative effectively. By prioritizing resources and aligning them with strategic objectives, organizations can ensure that implementation efforts receive the support and attention they require to succeed.

cssCopy code

```
$ resource_allocation_plan --execute
```

Continuous Monitoring and Improvement: Continuous monitoring and improvement are critical for overcoming implementation hurdles and driving ongoing success. Organizations should establish mechanisms for monitoring progress, collecting feedback, and identifying areas for improvement throughout the implementation process. By regularly evaluating performance, identifying lessons learned, and making iterative improvements, organizations can adapt to evolving circumstances and enhance the effectiveness of their implementation efforts. cssCopy code

```
$ continuous_improvement_process --implement
```

In summary, strategies for overcoming implementation hurdles involve proactive planning, effective communication, stakeholder engagement, training and development, flexibility and adaptability, resource allocation and management, and continuous monitoring and improvement. By employing these strategies, organizations can navigate challenges more effectively and increase the likelihood of successful implementation of their initiatives, ultimately driving positive outcomes and achieving their strategic objectives.

Chapter 9: Aligning KPIs with Business Objectives

The importance of aligning key performance indicators (KPIs) with organizational goals cannot be overstated in the context of effective performance measurement and management. KPIs serve as critical metrics that organizations use to assess progress, evaluate performance, and drive strategic decision-making. However, for KPIs to fulfill their intended purpose and deliver value to the organization, they must be directly aligned with organizational goals and objectives. This alignment ensures that KPIs reflect the priorities and strategic direction of the organization, guiding efforts towards the achievement of overarching objectives and contributing to organizational success.

Aligning KPIs with organizational goals serves several important purposes. First and foremost, it ensures that performance measurement efforts are focused on areas that are most critical to the organization's success. By identifying and prioritizing key strategic objectives, organizations can define KPIs that directly reflect these priorities, providing meaningful insights into progress towards achieving them. This alignment helps organizations avoid the common pitfall of measuring irrelevant or non-strategic metrics that do not contribute to overall success.

To align KPIs with organizational goals effectively, organizations must first establish clear and measurable objectives that reflect their strategic priorities. These objectives should be specific, achievable, relevant, and time-bound, providing a clear framework for performance measurement and management. Once objectives are defined, organizations can then identify the most relevant KPIs that will allow them to track progress towards these objectives accurately.

Aligning KPIs with organizational goals also enhances accountability and transparency within the organization. When KPIs are directly tied to strategic objectives, it becomes clear how individual and team performance contributes to overall organizational success. This transparency fosters a sense of accountability among employees, motivating them to align their efforts with organizational goals and take ownership of their contributions to achieving them.

Moreover, alignment between KPIs and organizational goals facilitates better decision-making at all levels of the organization. By providing clear visibility into performance relative to strategic objectives, KPIs enable leaders to identify areas of strength and weakness, allocate resources effectively, and make informed decisions to drive performance improvement. For example, if a KPI related to customer satisfaction is aligned with the organization's goal of improving customer retention, leaders can use insights from this KPI to identify opportunities for enhancing customer service and loyalty.

In addition to driving strategic alignment and accountability, aligning KPIs with organizational goals helps foster a culture of continuous improvement within the organization. When KPIs are directly tied to strategic objectives, organizations can use performance data to identify trends, analyze root causes of performance issues, and implement targeted improvement initiatives. This continuous improvement cycle enables organizations to adapt to changing market conditions, seize opportunities for growth, and stay ahead of the competition.

To align KPIs with organizational goals effectively, organizations must ensure ongoing communication and collaboration across all levels of the organization. Leaders should clearly communicate strategic objectives and the rationale behind selected KPIs to ensure buy-in and alignment among employees. Regular reviews and discussions about KPI performance should be conducted to evaluate progress, identify challenges, and adjust strategies as needed to stay on track towards achieving organizational goals.

Moreover, organizations should leverage technology and data analytics tools to track, monitor, and analyze KPI performance effectively. By investing in robust performance management systems, organizations can automate data collection processes, generate real-time insights, and visualize performance trends to inform decision-making and drive continuous improvement efforts.

In summary, the importance of aligning KPIs with organizational goals cannot be overstated in the context of effective performance measurement and management. By ensuring that KPIs reflect strategic priorities, organizations can focus their efforts on areas that are most critical to success, enhance accountability and transparency, facilitate better decision-making, foster a culture of continuous improvement, and ultimately achieve their strategic objectives.

Ensuring that key performance indicators (KPIs) support business objectives is paramount for organizations striving for success in today's competitive landscape. KPIs serve as vital tools for measuring progress, guiding decision-making, and driving performance improvement initiatives. However, to effectively support business objectives, KPIs must be carefully selected, aligned with strategic priorities, and regularly reviewed to ensure relevance and effectiveness. Several techniques can be employed to ensure that KPIs effectively support business objectives, ranging from establishing clear objectives and KPI selection criteria to implementing robust monitoring and evaluation processes.

Establish Clear Objectives: The first step in ensuring that KPIs support business objectives is to establish clear and measurable objectives that align with the organization's strategic priorities. Objectives should be specific, achievable, relevant, and time-bound (SMART), providing a clear roadmap for performance measurement and management. By defining clear objectives, organizations can identify the most relevant KPIs that will enable them to track progress towards achieving these objectives effectively.

shellCopy code

```shell
$ echo "Establish clear and measurable objectives that align with strategic priorities."
```

Define KPI Selection Criteria: Once objectives are established, organizations should define criteria for selecting KPIs that are directly aligned with business objectives. KPI selection criteria should consider factors such as relevance, measurability, attainability, and alignment with strategic priorities. By establishing clear selection criteria, organizations can ensure that KPIs are chosen based on their ability to provide meaningful insights into progress towards achieving business objectives.

perlCopy code

```
$ grep -i "KPI selection criteria" KPI_selection_criteria_document.txt
```

Align KPIs with Business Objectives: Selected KPIs should be directly aligned with business objectives to ensure that they effectively support strategic priorities. Each KPI should have a clear link to a specific business objective, enabling organizations to track performance in key areas of importance. By aligning KPIs with business objectives, organizations can focus their efforts on areas that are most critical to achieving success and drive performance improvement initiatives accordingly.

cssCopy code

```
$ align_KPIs_with_objectives --execute
```

Prioritize KPIs Based on Importance: Not all KPIs are created equal, and organizations should prioritize KPIs based on their importance in supporting business objectives. High-priority KPIs should receive more attention and resources, as they directly impact strategic priorities and organizational success. By prioritizing KPIs, organizations can ensure that resources are allocated effectively and efforts are focused on areas that will have the greatest impact on achieving business objectives.

cssCopy code

```
$ prioritize_KPIs --high-priority
```

Regularly Review and Evaluate KPIs: To ensure that KPIs continue to support business objectives effectively, organizations should establish processes for regular review and evaluation of KPI performance. Regular reviews enable organizations to assess the relevance, accuracy, and effectiveness of KPIs in measuring progress towards business objectives. By identifying gaps or areas for improvement, organizations can make informed decisions to adjust KPIs as needed to better align with evolving business priorities.

rubyCopy code

```
$ KPI_performance_review --schedule "Monthly"
```

Foster Cross-Functional Collaboration: Effective KPI management requires collaboration across different departments and functions within the organization. By involving key stakeholders from various areas of the business in the KPI selection and review process, organizations can ensure that KPIs are relevant and meaningful to all parts of the organization. Cross-functional collaboration fosters alignment and buy-in, facilitating the effective use of KPIs to support business objectives.

sqlCopy code

```
$ cross-functional_collaboration --engage
```

Leverage Technology and Data Analytics: Technology plays a crucial role in ensuring that KPIs support business objectives effectively. Organizations should leverage technology and data analytics tools to collect, analyze, and visualize KPI data in real-time. By investing in robust performance management systems, organizations can gain actionable insights into performance trends, identify areas for improvement, and make data-driven decisions to drive business success.

rubyCopy code

```
$ deploy_performance_management_system
```

In summary, ensuring that KPIs effectively support business objectives requires careful planning, alignment, and ongoing evaluation. By establishing clear objectives, defining selection criteria, aligning KPIs with business objectives, prioritizing KPIs, regularly reviewing and evaluating performance, fostering cross-functional collaboration, and leveraging technology and data analytics, organizations can maximize the value of KPIs in driving performance improvement and achieving strategic goals.

Chapter 10: Case Studies: Successful KPI Implementation in Service Desk Management

Real-world examples of successful key performance indicator (KPI) implementations provide valuable insights into how organizations leverage KPIs to drive performance improvement and achieve their strategic objectives. These success stories illustrate the diverse applications of KPIs across different industries and highlight the tangible benefits that organizations can realize through effective KPI management. From increased operational efficiency to enhanced customer satisfaction, these examples demonstrate the transformative impact of KPIs in driving organizational success.

Netflix: One of the most prominent examples of KPI implementation success is Netflix, the global streaming giant. Netflix utilizes a variety of KPIs to track user engagement, content performance, and subscriber growth. One key KPI that Netflix closely monitors is subscriber retention rate, which measures the percentage of subscribers who continue to renew their subscriptions over time. By analyzing this KPI, Netflix can identify factors that influence subscriber churn and take proactive measures to retain customers, such as investing in original content and personalizing recommendations.

cssCopy code

```
$ netflix_KPI_analysis --subscribers --retention_rate
```

Amazon: Amazon is another example of a company that has successfully leveraged KPIs to drive business growth and innovation. Amazon tracks a wide range of KPIs related to customer satisfaction, order fulfillment, and operational efficiency. One notable KPI is the "click-to-ship" time, which measures the time it takes for an order to be processed and shipped after it is placed. By continuously optimizing this KPI, Amazon has been able to streamline its fulfillment processes and deliver orders to customers faster, leading to higher levels of customer satisfaction and loyalty.

cssCopy code

```
$ amazon_KPI_optimization --click_to_ship_time
```

Tesla: Tesla, the electric vehicle manufacturer, is known for its innovative approach to KPI management. Tesla closely monitors KPIs related to vehicle production, quality control, and sales performance to ensure operational excellence and meet customer demand. One key KPI that Tesla focuses on is the production yield rate, which measures the percentage of defect-free vehicles produced during manufacturing. By maintaining a high production yield rate, Tesla can minimize production costs and deliver high-quality vehicles to customers, enhancing brand reputation and customer satisfaction.

cssCopy code

```
$ tesla_KPI_monitoring --production_yield_rate
```

Starbucks: Starbucks, the global coffee chain, utilizes KPIs to drive performance improvement across its retail operations. Starbucks tracks KPIs related to store traffic, customer satisfaction, and product sales to optimize

store performance and enhance the customer experience. One critical KPI for Starbucks is the average transaction value, which measures the average amount spent by customers during each visit. By analyzing this KPI, Starbucks can identify opportunities to upsell or cross-sell products and increase overall sales revenue.
cssCopy code

```
$ starbucks_KPI_analysis --average_transaction_value
```

Airbnb: Airbnb, the online marketplace for lodging and vacation rentals, relies on KPIs to measure host and guest satisfaction, property performance, and booking conversion rates. One key KPI for Airbnb is the host response rate, which measures the percentage of inquiries from guests that receive a timely response from hosts. By encouraging hosts to maintain a high response rate, Airbnb can enhance the overall guest experience and improve booking conversion rates, leading to increased revenue and customer loyalty.
cssCopy code

```
$ airbnb_KPI_tracking --host_response_rate
```

Walmart: As one of the world's largest retailers, Walmart utilizes KPIs to optimize store operations, supply chain management, and customer service. One notable KPI for Walmart is inventory turnover, which measures the rate at which inventory is sold and replaced over a specific period. By optimizing inventory turnover, Walmart can minimize carrying costs, reduce stockouts, and improve profitability. Additionally, Walmart tracks KPIs related to store performance, such as sales per square foot and customer satisfaction scores, to identify opportunities for improvement and enhance the overall shopping experience.

cssCopy code

```
$ walmart_KPI_optimization --inventory_turnover
```

Spotify: Spotify, the leading music streaming service, relies on KPIs to measure user engagement, content performance, and subscription growth. One key KPI for Spotify is monthly active users (MAUs), which measures the number of unique users who engage with the platform each month. By tracking MAUs and other engagement metrics, Spotify can assess the popularity of its platform, identify trends in user behavior, and tailor its content recommendations and marketing strategies to drive user retention and acquisition.

cssCopy code

```
$ spotify_KPI_tracking --monthly_active_users
```

In summary, these real-world examples of KPI implementation success stories demonstrate the diverse applications and benefits of KPIs across different industries. From streaming services to retail giants, organizations leverage KPIs to drive operational excellence, enhance customer satisfaction, and achieve strategic objectives. By effectively monitoring and analyzing KPIs, organizations can gain valuable insights into performance trends, identify areas for improvement, and make data-driven decisions to drive business success.

Lessons learned and best practices from case studies provide invaluable insights into the real-world application of techniques and strategies across various domains. Analyzing case studies allows us to glean actionable lessons, identify common challenges, and extract best practices that can be applied to similar situations. By examining successful case studies, organizations can learn from others' experiences, avoid pitfalls, and enhance their own performance. Here are some lessons learned and best practices distilled from a selection of case studies across different industries:

Clear Objectives are Essential: In numerous case studies, the importance of having clear objectives emerged as a common theme. Organizations that articulated specific, measurable, achievable, relevant, and time-bound (SMART) objectives were better positioned to drive success. For instance, companies like Netflix and Amazon set clear objectives related to customer retention and operational efficiency, guiding their KPI selection and management efforts.

cssCopy code

```
$ grep -i "clear objectives" case_study.txt
```

Alignment with Business Goals: Successful organizations consistently aligned their initiatives with overarching business goals. Whether it was Tesla's focus on production yield rate to ensure quality or Starbucks' emphasis on average transaction value to drive revenue, aligning KPIs with business objectives proved crucial for achieving desired outcomes.

perlCopy code

```
$ grep -i "alignment with business goals" case_study.txt
```

Continuous Monitoring and Adaptation: Case studies highlighted the importance of continuous monitoring and adaptation in response to changing circumstances.

Organizations that regularly reviewed their performance against KPIs and adjusted strategies accordingly were more agile and resilient. Walmart's optimization of inventory turnover and Spotify's tracking of monthly active users exemplify this approach.

rubyCopy code

```
$ continuous_monitoring_and_adaptation --schedule "monthly"
```

Data-Driven Decision Making: Data-driven decision-making emerged as a best practice across multiple case studies. Organizations that leveraged data analytics to derive insights and guide decision-making were able to make informed choices and drive performance improvement. Airbnb's emphasis on host response rates and Spotify's analysis of user engagement metrics exemplify this best practice.

cssCopy code

```
$ data_driven_decision_making --analyze
```

Cross-Functional Collaboration: Effective collaboration across different functions within organizations was a common thread in successful case studies. Cross-functional teams that collaborated closely on KPI selection, monitoring, and evaluation were better equipped to achieve shared goals. Amazon's optimization of click-to-ship time and Starbucks' focus on store performance metrics are examples of successful cross-functional collaboration.

sqlCopy code

```
$ cross-functional_collaboration --engage
```

Customer-Centric Focus: Organizations that prioritized the customer experience consistently outperformed their peers. By measuring and optimizing KPIs related to customer satisfaction and engagement, companies like Netflix, Amazon, and Airbnb were able to enhance customer loyalty and drive business growth.

perlCopy code

```
$ grep -i "customer-centric focus" case_study.txt
```

Continuous Improvement Culture: Cultivating a culture of continuous improvement was instrumental in the success of many organizations. By encouraging experimentation, innovation, and learning from failures, companies like Netflix, Tesla, and Spotify were able to stay ahead of the curve and adapt to evolving market dynamics.

cssCopy code

```
$ continuous_improvement_culture --promote
```

In summary, lessons learned and best practices from case studies provide valuable guidance for organizations seeking to drive performance improvement and achieve their strategic objectives. By adopting clear objectives, aligning initiatives with business goals, embracing continuous monitoring and adaptation, leveraging data-driven decision-making, fostering cross-functional collaboration, prioritizing the customer experience, and cultivating a culture of continuous improvement, organizations can increase their likelihood of success in today's dynamic business environment.

BOOK 3
SLA MASTERY
ADVANCED STRATEGIES FOR SERVICE DESK MANAGERS

ROB BOTWRIGHT

Chapter 1: Understanding Service Level Agreements (SLAs)

Service Level Agreements (SLAs) play a pivotal role in service desk operations, serving as contractual agreements between service providers and customers that define the level of service expected and the metrics by which that service will be measured. The purpose and importance of SLAs cannot be overstated, as they provide a framework for ensuring accountability, establishing clear expectations, and driving continuous improvement in service delivery. SLAs are essential in service desk operations for several reasons, including facilitating effective communication, prioritizing tasks, managing customer expectations, and enhancing overall service quality.

SLAs serve as a vital communication tool between service providers and customers, clarifying the scope of services offered, the responsibilities of each party, and the metrics used to measure performance. By clearly defining these parameters, SLAs help to align expectations and minimize misunderstandings, ensuring that both parties have a shared understanding of what constitutes acceptable service levels. This clarity is essential for building trust and maintaining positive relationships with customers, as it fosters transparency and accountability in service delivery.

perlCopy code

```
$ grep -i "service level agreements" documentation.txt
```

Moreover, SLAs play a crucial role in prioritizing tasks and allocating resources effectively within the service desk environment. By establishing service level targets for different types of incidents and requests, SLAs help service desk teams to prioritize their workload based on the urgency and impact of each issue. This enables them to focus their efforts on resolving critical issues promptly while ensuring that less urgent tasks are addressed in a timely manner. As a result, SLAs contribute to the efficient use of resources and help to minimize disruptions to business operations.

```css
cssCopy code
$ prioritize_tasks --based_on_SLAs
```

In addition to facilitating communication and task prioritization, SLAs also play a key role in managing customer expectations. By clearly defining the expected response times, resolution times, and service availability levels, SLAs help to set realistic expectations for customers regarding the level of service they can expect to receive. This transparency is essential for building customer confidence and satisfaction, as it ensures that customers know what to expect and can plan accordingly. When service levels meet or exceed expectations, customers are more likely to perceive the service desk as responsive, reliable, and customer-focused.

```css
cssCopy code
$ manage_customer_expectations --based_on_SLAs
```

Furthermore, SLAs are instrumental in driving continuous improvement in service delivery by providing a framework for monitoring and measuring performance. By tracking key performance indicators (KPIs) outlined in the SLAs, service desk managers can identify areas where performance falls short of the agreed-upon targets and take corrective action to address any deficiencies. This ongoing monitoring and evaluation process enables service desk teams to identify trends, identify recurring issues, and implement process improvements to enhance overall service quality and efficiency over time.

cssCopy code

```
$ monitor_performance_metrics --outlined_in_SLAs
```

In summary, the purpose and importance of SLAs in service desk operations cannot be overstated. SLAs serve as a critical communication tool, facilitating effective communication between service providers and customers, prioritizing tasks, managing customer expectations, and driving continuous improvement in service delivery. By establishing clear expectations, defining service levels, and providing a framework for monitoring and measuring performance, SLAs help to ensure that service desk operations are efficient, responsive, and customer-focused. As such, SLAs are essential for maintaining high levels of customer satisfaction and delivering value to the organization.

The components and structure of Service Level Agreements (SLAs) are crucial for defining the terms and conditions of service delivery between service providers and customers. Understanding these components and their structure is essential for creating effective SLAs that meet the needs of both parties involved. A typical SLA comprises several key components, including service scope, service metrics, performance targets, roles and responsibilities, escalation procedures, and governance mechanisms. Each of these components plays a specific role in shaping the structure and content of the SLA, ensuring that it accurately reflects the expectations and requirements of both parties.

The service scope is the first component of an SLA and outlines the services that will be provided by the service provider. This section typically includes a detailed description of the services offered, along with any exclusions or limitations. By clearly defining the scope of services, the SLA sets expectations regarding the types of services that will be delivered and the boundaries of service provision.

rubyCopy code

```
$ define_service_scope --description "services offered" --exclusions "limitations"
```

The next component of an SLA is the service metrics, which define the specific metrics that will be used to measure the performance of the service provider. These metrics may include response times, resolution times, uptime percentages, and other key performance indicators (KPIs) relevant to the services being provided. By establishing clear metrics, the SLA provides a basis for objectively evaluating the quality of service delivery and holding the service provider accountable for meeting performance targets.

cssCopy code

```
$ define_service_metrics --response_times --resolution_times --uptime_percentages
```

Performance targets are another critical component of an SLA and specify the desired level of performance for each service metric. These targets may be expressed as numerical values, percentages, or qualitative descriptions, depending on the nature of the metric. Setting realistic and achievable performance targets is essential for ensuring that the SLA is meaningful and actionable, as overly ambitious targets may be difficult or impossible to meet in practice.

rubyCopy code

```ruby
$ set_performance_targets --response_times "within 1 hour" --resolution_times "within 4 hours" --uptime_percentages "99.9%"
```

Roles and responsibilities outline the responsibilities of each party involved in the SLA, including the service provider, the customer, and any third-party vendors or suppliers. This section defines who is responsible for performing specific tasks, resolving issues, and communicating with stakeholders. Clearly defining roles and responsibilities helps to ensure accountability and avoid misunderstandings or disputes regarding the division of labor.

cssCopy code

```css
$ define_roles_and_responsibilities --service_provider --customer --third_party_vendors
```

Escalation procedures outline the process for escalating issues or complaints that cannot be resolved at the operational level. This section typically includes a hierarchical escalation path, specifying who should be contacted in the event of a service outage, performance degradation, or other significant issues. By providing a clear escalation process, the SLA ensures that problems are addressed promptly and effectively, minimizing the impact on service delivery.

cssCopy code

```css
$ outline_escalation_procedures --hierarchical_path --contacts
```

Finally, governance mechanisms establish the framework for monitoring and managing the SLA, including procedures for reviewing performance, enforcing compliance, and resolving disputes. This section may include provisions for regular performance reviews, service level reporting, service credits or penalties for non-compliance, and mechanisms for resolving disagreements between the parties. Governance mechanisms are essential for ensuring that the SLA remains effective and relevant over time, as they provide a framework for managing the ongoing relationship between the service provider and the customer.

cssCopy code

```
$         establish_governance_mechanisms         --
performance_reviews      --service_level_reporting      --
dispute_resolution
```

In summary, the components and structure of SLAs are essential for defining the terms and conditions of service delivery and ensuring that the expectations of both parties are clearly defined and understood. By including key components such as service scope, service metrics, performance targets, roles and responsibilities, escalation procedures, and governance mechanisms, SLAs provide a comprehensive framework for managing the relationship between service providers and customers. Understanding these components and their structure is critical for creating effective SLAs that support the delivery of high-quality services and facilitate positive outcomes for all parties involved.

Chapter 2: Defining SLA Metrics and Targets

Key Performance Indicators (KPIs) are critical metrics used to evaluate the performance and effectiveness of services provided under Service Level Agreements (SLAs). Within SLAs, KPIs serve as benchmarks against which the service provider's performance is measured, providing valuable insights into the quality and efficiency of service delivery. These KPIs are carefully selected to align with the objectives and expectations outlined in the SLA and are essential for monitoring, assessing, and optimizing service performance. Understanding the role and significance of KPIs within SLAs is crucial for both service providers and customers, as they provide valuable insights into the health of the service relationship and drive continuous improvement efforts.

KPIs in SLAs encompass a wide range of metrics that span various aspects of service delivery, including responsiveness, efficiency, reliability, and customer satisfaction. These metrics are selected based on their relevance to the specific services being provided and their ability to accurately reflect the quality of service. Common KPIs found in SLAs include response time, resolution time, uptime/downtime, service availability, first contact resolution rate, customer satisfaction score (CSAT), and adherence to service level targets.

perlCopy code

```
$ grep -i "Key Performance Indicators (KPIs)"
glossary.txt
```

Response time is one of the most critical KPIs in SLAs, measuring the time taken by the service provider to respond to a customer request or incident. This metric is crucial for assessing the responsiveness of the service desk and ensuring timely assistance for customers. Response time targets are typically defined in the SLA and may vary depending on the severity and urgency of the issue.

cssCopy code

```
$ measure_response_time --service_desk
```

Resolution time measures the time taken by the service provider to resolve a customer request or incident from the moment it is reported until it is fully resolved. This KPI is essential for evaluating the efficiency and effectiveness of the service desk in addressing customer issues promptly and effectively. Resolution time targets are typically established based on the severity and complexity of the issue and are outlined in the SLA.

cssCopy code

```
$ measure_resolution_time --service_desk
```

Uptime and downtime are KPIs that measure the availability and reliability of the services provided. Uptime refers to the percentage of time that services are available and accessible to users, while downtime represents the periods when services are unavailable or experiencing disruptions. These metrics are critical for assessing service reliability and ensuring that service level targets for availability are met as per the SLA.

cssCopy code

```
$ measure_uptime --service_availability
```

First contact resolution rate measures the percentage of customer issues or requests that are resolved during the initial contact with the service desk, without the need for further escalation or follow-up. This KPI is indicative of the service desk's efficiency and capability in addressing customer issues promptly and minimizing customer effort. A high first contact resolution rate is often considered a sign of effective service delivery.

cssCopy code

```
$ measure_first_contact_resolution_rate --service_desk
```

Customer satisfaction score (CSAT) is a KPI that measures the level of satisfaction or dissatisfaction among customers with the services provided. CSAT surveys are commonly used to collect feedback from customers regarding their service experience, and the results are used to calculate a satisfaction score. This metric is vital for gauging customer perceptions and identifying areas for improvement in service delivery.

cssCopy code

```
$ measure_customer_satisfaction_score --CSAT_survey
```

Adherence to service level targets is a KPI that measures the service provider's compliance with the performance targets outlined in the SLA. This metric evaluates whether the service provider is meeting the agreed-upon service levels for response time, resolution time, uptime, and other performance indicators. Adherence to service level targets is crucial for ensuring accountability and maintaining trust between the service provider and the customer.

csscopy code

$ measure_adherence_to_service_level_targets --SLA

In summary, Key Performance Indicators (KPIs) play a vital role in Service Level Agreements (SLAs) by providing objective measures to evaluate the performance and effectiveness of service delivery. These KPIs encompass various metrics related to responsiveness, efficiency, reliability, and customer satisfaction, and are essential for monitoring, assessing, and optimizing service performance. Understanding the significance of KPIs within SLAs is crucial for both service providers and customers, as they provide valuable insights into the health of the service relationship and drive continuous improvement efforts.

Setting measurable targets for service levels is a critical aspect of Service Level Management (SLM) and plays a fundamental role in ensuring the delivery of high-quality services that meet the expectations of customers and stakeholders. These targets serve as benchmarks against which the performance of service providers is evaluated, providing clear criteria for assessing service performance and driving continuous improvement efforts. The process of setting measurable targets involves defining specific, quantifiable objectives for various aspects of service delivery, including response times, resolution times, uptime/downtime, and other key performance indicators (KPIs) outlined in the Service Level Agreement (SLA). By establishing clear and achievable targets, organizations can effectively monitor and manage service performance, identify areas for improvement, and demonstrate their commitment to meeting customer needs and requirements.

The first step in setting measurable targets for service levels is to identify the key performance indicators (KPIs) that are most relevant to the services being provided and align with the goals and objectives outlined in the SLA. These KPIs may vary depending on the nature of the services, industry standards, regulatory requirements, and customer expectations. Common KPIs include response time, resolution time, uptime/downtime, service availability, first contact resolution rate, and customer satisfaction score (CSAT).

cssCopy code

```
$        identify_key_performance_indicators        --
services_provided
```

Once the relevant KPIs have been identified, the next step is to define specific targets or objectives for each metric, taking into account factors such as service level requirements, customer expectations, business priorities, and resource constraints. These targets should be realistic, measurable, achievable, relevant, and time-bound (SMART), ensuring that they are both meaningful and actionable.

shellCopy code

```
$ define_targets --response_time "within 2 hours" --
resolution_time "within 4 hours" --uptime "99.9%"
```

When defining targets for response time, organizations may consider factors such as the urgency and severity of the request, the complexity of the issue, and the availability of resources. For example, high-priority incidents may have shorter response time targets compared to lower-priority requests, reflecting their greater impact on business operations.

cssCopy code

```
$ define_response_time_targets --priority --severity --resources
```

Resolution time targets should similarly take into account the complexity of the issue, the level of effort required to resolve it, and any dependencies or constraints that may impact resolution time. Organizations may establish different resolution time targets for different types of incidents or service requests, ensuring that targets are tailored to the specific needs of each customer or service offering.

cssCopy code

```
$ define_resolution_time_targets --complexity --effort --dependencies
```

Uptime targets define the minimum acceptable level of service availability and reliability, reflecting the organization's commitment to maintaining service continuity and minimizing disruptions. These targets may be expressed as a percentage of uptime over a specified time period (e.g., 99.9% uptime per month) and should take into account factors such as planned maintenance, system upgrades, and unforeseen outages.

cssCopy code

```
$ define_uptime_targets --percentage --time_period --planned_maintenance
```

Service level targets should be periodically reviewed and updated as needed to ensure they remain relevant and aligned with changing business requirements, customer expectations, and industry standards. Regular performance monitoring and reporting are essential for tracking progress towards targets, identifying areas for improvement, and addressing any deviations or discrepancies in service performance.

cssCopy code

```
$              review_and_update_targets         --
performance_monitoring         --reporting         --
continuous_improvement
```

In summary, setting measurable targets for service levels is a critical aspect of Service Level Management (SLM) and plays a key role in ensuring the delivery of high-quality services that meet the expectations of customers and stakeholders. By defining specific, quantifiable objectives for key performance indicators (KPIs) such as response time, resolution time, and uptime/downtime, organizations can effectively monitor and manage service performance, drive continuous improvement efforts, and demonstrate their commitment to meeting customer needs and requirements.

Chapter 3: Negotiating SLAs with Stakeholders

Strategies for effective stakeholder engagement in SLA negotiations are crucial for ensuring the successful development and implementation of Service Level Agreements (SLAs) that meet the needs and expectations of all parties involved. Effective stakeholder engagement fosters collaboration, communication, and alignment of interests, leading to the establishment of mutually beneficial agreements that support the achievement of business objectives and customer satisfaction. These strategies involve identifying key stakeholders, understanding their interests and priorities, facilitating open and transparent communication, negotiating win-win solutions, and establishing mechanisms for ongoing collaboration and review.

The first step in effective stakeholder engagement is to identify all relevant stakeholders who have a vested interest in the SLA negotiation process and the services being provided. These stakeholders may include internal departments, external vendors or service providers, customers, and other business units or partners. By identifying key stakeholders upfront, organizations can ensure that all perspectives and interests are considered during the negotiation process and that potential conflicts or issues are addressed proactively.

cssCopy code

```
$ identify_stakeholders --SLA_negotiation_process
```

Once stakeholders have been identified, the next step is to understand their interests, priorities, and concerns related to the SLA negotiation. This may involve conducting stakeholder interviews, surveys, or workshops to gather input and feedback on key issues and requirements. By understanding the needs and expectations of stakeholders, organizations can tailor their negotiation strategies and proposals to address specific concerns and maximize buy-in and support.

cssCopy code

```
$ gather_stakeholder_input --interviews --surveys --workshops
```

Facilitating open and transparent communication is essential for building trust and fostering collaboration among stakeholders during the SLA negotiation process. Organizations should establish clear channels for communication, such as regular meetings, status updates, and feedback sessions, to ensure that stakeholders are kept informed and involved throughout the process. Additionally, organizations should provide opportunities for stakeholders to ask questions, raise concerns, and provide input to ensure that their perspectives are heard and considered.

cssCopy code

```
$ facilitate_communication --regular_meetings --status_updates --feedback_sessions
```

Negotiating win-win solutions involves finding common ground and reaching agreements that benefit all parties involved in the SLA negotiation. This may require compromise and flexibility on the part of both service providers and customers to ensure that the final agreement meets the needs and objectives of all stakeholders. By focusing on mutual interests and shared goals, organizations can build trust and collaboration among stakeholders and create agreements that are sustainable and effective in achieving desired outcomes.

cssCopy code

```
$ negotiate_win_win_solutions --compromise --flexibility --mutual_interests
```

Establishing mechanisms for ongoing collaboration and review is essential for ensuring that SLAs remain relevant and effective over time. Organizations should define clear roles and responsibilities for stakeholders, establish processes for monitoring and evaluating SLA performance, and implement mechanisms for addressing issues or changes as they arise. By maintaining open lines of communication and regularly reviewing SLA performance, organizations can identify opportunities for improvement and continuously optimize service delivery to meet evolving needs and expectations.

cssCopy code

```
$ establish_collaboration_mechanisms --monitoring --evaluation --issue_resolution
```

In summary, strategies for effective stakeholder engagement in SLA negotiations are essential for ensuring the successful development and implementation of Service Level Agreements (SLAs) that meet the needs and expectations of all parties involved. By identifying key stakeholders, understanding their interests and priorities, facilitating open and transparent communication, negotiating win-win solutions, and establishing mechanisms for ongoing collaboration and review, organizations can create agreements that support the achievement of business objectives and customer satisfaction. Effective stakeholder engagement fosters collaboration, communication, and alignment of interests, leading to the establishment of mutually beneficial agreements that drive business success and customer value.

Balancing stakeholder expectations with feasibility is a critical aspect of project management and organizational leadership, requiring a delicate equilibrium between meeting the needs and desires of stakeholders and ensuring that projects are realistic, achievable, and sustainable. This balancing act involves understanding the diverse perspectives and interests of stakeholders, assessing the technical, financial, and resource constraints of projects, and aligning expectations with available capabilities and constraints. By adopting a collaborative and transparent approach, leveraging stakeholder engagement techniques, and prioritizing realistic goals and objectives, organizations can effectively navigate the complexities of balancing stakeholder expectations with feasibility and drive successful project outcomes.

Understanding the diverse perspectives and interests of stakeholders is essential for identifying potential conflicts or discrepancies between stakeholder expectations and project feasibility. Stakeholders may include internal and external parties with varying priorities, preferences, and objectives, such as customers, end-users, project sponsors, team members, and regulatory bodies. Conducting stakeholder analysis and engaging stakeholders early in the project lifecycle can help organizations gain insights into their needs, concerns, and expectations, enabling them to proactively address potential issues and align project goals with stakeholder interests.

cssCopy code

```
$ stakeholder_analysis --identify_interests --priorities --concerns
```

Assessing the technical, financial, and resource constraints of projects is crucial for determining the feasibility of meeting stakeholder expectations within available capabilities. This may involve conducting feasibility studies, risk assessments, and impact analyses to evaluate the technical complexity, financial viability, and resource requirements of proposed initiatives. By quantifying risks and constraints and considering alternative approaches or mitigation strategies, organizations can develop realistic project plans that balance stakeholder expectations with feasibility.

cssCopy code

```
$ conduct_feasibility_studies --technical --financial --resource_constraints
```

Aligning expectations with available capabilities and constraints requires open and transparent communication with stakeholders to manage their expectations effectively. Organizations should communicate clearly and honestly about the limitations and trade-offs associated with projects, providing stakeholders with realistic assessments of what can be achieved within given constraints. By setting clear expectations upfront and managing stakeholder perceptions throughout the project lifecycle, organizations can minimize the likelihood of misunderstandings or conflicts arising due to unmet expectations.

cssCopy code

```
$ communicate_expectations --clearly --honestly --transparently
```

Adopting a collaborative and inclusive approach to stakeholder engagement can help organizations balance diverse perspectives and interests and foster a sense of ownership and accountability among stakeholders. By involving stakeholders in decision-making processes, soliciting their input and feedback, and empowering them to contribute to project planning and execution, organizations can harness the collective wisdom and expertise of stakeholders to drive informed and effective decision-making and build consensus around project goals and objectives.

cssCopy code

```
$ adopt_collaborative_approach --inclusive_engagement --decision_making --feedback
```

Prioritizing realistic goals and objectives is essential for ensuring that projects remain feasible and achievable within given constraints. Organizations should prioritize initiatives based on their strategic importance, potential impact, and alignment with organizational goals and objectives, focusing on initiatives that offer the greatest value and return on investment. By setting achievable milestones and deliverables and breaking down projects into manageable tasks, organizations can maintain momentum and progress towards project goals while balancing stakeholder expectations with feasibility.

cssCopy code

```
$ prioritize_realistic_goals --strategic_importance --potential_impact --alignment
```

In summary, balancing stakeholder expectations with feasibility is a complex and multifaceted challenge that requires organizations to understand the diverse perspectives and interests of stakeholders, assess the technical, financial, and resource constraints of projects, align expectations with available capabilities and constraints, adopt a collaborative and inclusive approach to stakeholder engagement, and prioritize realistic goals and objectives. By leveraging stakeholder engagement techniques, communicating openly and transparently, and focusing on achievable outcomes, organizations can navigate the complexities of balancing stakeholder expectations with feasibility and drive successful project outcomes that meet the needs and expectations of all stakeholders involved.

Chapter 4: Monitoring and Reporting SLA Performance

Establishing monitoring processes for SLA compliance is essential for ensuring that service level agreements (SLAs) are effectively implemented and maintained. These processes involve defining key performance indicators (KPIs), establishing monitoring mechanisms, collecting relevant data, analyzing performance metrics, and taking corrective actions to address any deviations from agreed-upon service levels. By implementing robust monitoring processes, organizations can proactively identify and address issues, optimize service delivery, and maintain high levels of customer satisfaction and trust.

Defining key performance indicators (KPIs) is the first step in establishing monitoring processes for SLA compliance. KPIs are quantifiable metrics that measure the performance of services against agreed-upon standards and targets. Organizations should identify KPIs that are relevant, measurable, and aligned with the objectives and requirements outlined in SLAs. Common KPIs include response time, resolution time, uptime, availability, and customer satisfaction scores.

cssCopy code

```
$ define_KPIs --relevant --measurable --aligned_with_SLAs
```

Once KPIs have been defined, organizations need to establish monitoring mechanisms to track performance against these metrics. This may involve deploying monitoring tools and software systems that collect and analyze data in real-time, generate performance reports, and provide alerts or notifications when SLA targets are at risk of being breached. Additionally, organizations may implement manual monitoring processes, such as periodic audits or reviews, to ensure ongoing compliance with SLAs.

cssCopy code

```
$         establish_monitoring_mechanisms        --
monitoring_tools        --software_systems        --
manual_processes
```

Collecting relevant data is crucial for monitoring SLA compliance effectively. Organizations should identify sources of data that provide insights into service performance and gather data consistently and accurately. This may include data from service desk tickets, system logs, customer surveys, and performance reports. By collecting comprehensive and reliable data, organizations can gain a holistic view of service delivery and identify areas for improvement.

cssCopy code

```
$ collect_data --service_desk_tickets --system_logs --
customer_surveys --performance_reports
```

Analyzing performance metrics is essential for identifying trends, patterns, and areas of concern related to SLA compliance. Organizations should regularly review performance data to assess adherence to SLA targets, identify potential bottlenecks or inefficiencies, and detect any deviations from expected service levels. Data analysis techniques may include trend analysis, root cause analysis, and comparative benchmarking against industry standards or best practices.

cssCopy code

```
$ analyze_performance_metrics --trend_analysis --root_cause_analysis --comparative_benchmarking
```

Taking corrective actions is necessary when deviations from SLA targets are identified during the monitoring process. Organizations should establish procedures and protocols for addressing performance issues, such as escalating unresolved incidents, implementing service improvements, or renegotiating SLAs with stakeholders. By taking timely and appropriate corrective actions, organizations can mitigate the impact of service disruptions, improve service quality, and maintain compliance with SLAs.

cssCopy code

```
$ take_corrective_actions --escalate_incidents --implement_service_improvements --renegotiate_SLAs
```

In summary, establishing monitoring processes for SLA compliance is essential for ensuring that organizations meet their commitments to customers and stakeholders. By defining key performance indicators, establishing monitoring mechanisms, collecting relevant data, analyzing performance metrics, and taking corrective actions, organizations can proactively monitor service delivery, identify areas for improvement, and maintain high levels of customer satisfaction and trust. Effective monitoring processes enable organizations to optimize service delivery, minimize service disruptions, and drive continuous improvement in service quality and performance.

Creating comprehensive SLA performance reports is a critical aspect of managing service level agreements (SLAs) effectively, providing stakeholders with valuable insights into the performance of services, adherence to SLA targets, and areas for improvement. These reports play a vital role in fostering transparency, accountability, and communication between service providers and customers, enabling informed decision-making, identifying trends and patterns, and driving continuous improvement initiatives. By leveraging appropriate tools, collecting relevant data, analyzing performance metrics, and presenting findings in a clear and concise manner, organizations can create meaningful SLA performance reports that facilitate collaboration, trust, and alignment with stakeholders.

To begin creating comprehensive SLA performance reports, organizations need to identify the key stakeholders who will be involved in the report's review and decision-making process. Stakeholders may include service desk managers, IT executives, business leaders, and external customers or clients. Engaging stakeholders early in the report creation process ensures that their input and feedback are considered, and that the report's content and format align with their needs and expectations.

cssCopy code

```
$ identify_stakeholders --service_desk_managers --IT_executives --business_leaders --customers
```

Once stakeholders have been identified, organizations should determine the specific metrics and KPIs that will be included in the SLA performance report. These metrics should be relevant, measurable, and aligned with the objectives outlined in the SLAs. Common metrics may include response time, resolution time, uptime, availability, customer satisfaction scores, and SLA adherence rates. By selecting the most meaningful and impactful metrics, organizations can provide stakeholders with actionable insights into service performance and compliance.

cssCopy code

```
$ determine_metrics --response_time --resolution_time --uptime --availability --customer_satisfaction --SLA_adherence
```

Next, organizations need to establish data collection mechanisms to gather the necessary information for the SLA performance report. This may involve deploying monitoring tools, data collection systems, and reporting software that capture performance data from various sources, such as service desk tickets, system logs, customer feedback surveys, and performance monitoring dashboards. By automating data collection processes and ensuring data accuracy and consistency, organizations can streamline the reporting process and produce reliable and actionable insights.

cssCopy code

```
$ establish_data_collection_mechanisms --monitoring_tools --data_collection_systems --reporting_software
```

With data collection mechanisms in place, organizations can begin collecting relevant performance data according to the predetermined metrics and KPIs. Data should be collected consistently and regularly to provide stakeholders with up-to-date information on service performance trends and patterns. Additionally, organizations may need to clean and preprocess data to remove duplicates, errors, or outliers that could skew the accuracy of the report's findings.

cssCopy code

```
$ collect_performance_data --consistently --regularly --clean_and_preprocess_data
```

Once the necessary data has been collected, organizations should analyze performance metrics to identify trends, patterns, and areas for improvement. This analysis may involve conducting trend analysis, root cause analysis, and comparative benchmarking against industry standards or best practices. By examining performance data from different perspectives, organizations can gain a deeper understanding of service performance and make informed decisions to drive continuous improvement initiatives.

cssCopy code

```
$ analyze_performance_metrics --trend_analysis --root_cause_analysis --comparative_benchmarking
```

After analyzing performance metrics, organizations can begin compiling the SLA performance report, presenting findings in a clear and concise manner that is easily understandable to stakeholders. The report should include an executive summary that highlights key insights and trends, followed by detailed performance data and analysis for each metric and KPI. Visualizations such as charts, graphs, and tables can help convey complex information effectively and enhance stakeholder engagement.

cssCopy code

```
$          compile_SLA_performance_report          --
executive_summary    --detailed_performance_data    --
visualizations
```

Finally, organizations should distribute the SLA performance report to stakeholders and facilitate discussions or meetings to review findings, discuss implications, and identify action items for improvement. This collaborative approach encourages transparency, accountability, and alignment with stakeholders, fostering a culture of continuous improvement and driving positive outcomes for both service providers and customers.

cssCopy code

```
$ distribute_SLA_performance_report --stakeholders --
facilitate_discussions --identify_action_items
```

In summary, creating comprehensive SLA performance reports is essential for monitoring service performance, ensuring SLA compliance, and driving continuous improvement initiatives. By identifying stakeholders, determining relevant metrics, establishing data collection mechanisms, analyzing performance data, compiling insightful reports, and facilitating discussions with stakeholders, organizations can demonstrate transparency, accountability, and commitment to delivering high-quality services that meet the needs and expectations of customers and stakeholders. Effective SLA performance reporting fosters collaboration, trust, and alignment, ultimately leading to enhanced service delivery and customer satisfaction.

Chapter 5: Managing SLA Breaches and Escalations

Protocols for handling SLA violations are crucial for maintaining service quality, managing customer expectations, and preserving organizational reputation. When SLA violations occur, it is essential for service providers to respond promptly, communicate effectively with stakeholders, and take appropriate corrective actions to minimize the impact on service delivery and customer satisfaction. By establishing clear protocols, defining escalation procedures, and implementing mitigation strategies, organizations can effectively manage SLA violations and uphold their commitments to customers and stakeholders.

To begin with, organizations need to establish clear protocols for identifying and reporting SLA violations. This involves defining the criteria for what constitutes an SLA violation, such as missing response or resolution times, downtime exceeding agreed-upon thresholds, or failure to meet service availability targets. By clearly outlining these criteria, organizations can ensure consistency in identifying and addressing SLA violations across different service offerings and customer engagements.

```css
cssCopy code
$ establish_protocols --identify_SLA_violations --define_criteria
```

Once SLA violations are identified, organizations need to implement escalation procedures to ensure timely resolution and communication with stakeholders. This may involve defining escalation paths, assigning responsibility to specific individuals or teams for handling SLA violations, and establishing response time targets for escalating and resolving issues. By implementing clear escalation procedures, organizations can ensure that SLA violations are addressed promptly and effectively, minimizing the impact on service delivery and customer satisfaction.

cssCopy code

```
$ implement_escalation_procedures --define_paths --assign_responsibility --establish_response_time_targets
```

Communication is key when handling SLA violations, and organizations should have protocols in place for communicating with stakeholders, including customers, internal teams, and management. This may involve notifying affected parties of SLA violations, providing regular updates on the status of remediation efforts, and offering assurances and remedies to mitigate the impact on service delivery. By maintaining open and transparent communication channels, organizations can build trust with stakeholders and demonstrate their commitment to addressing SLA violations promptly and effectively.

cssCopy code

```
$ establish_communication_protocols --notify_stakeholders --provide_updates --offer_assurances
```

In addition to addressing SLA violations reactively, organizations should also implement proactive measures to prevent future violations and improve overall service quality. This may involve conducting root cause analysis to identify underlying issues contributing to SLA violations, implementing corrective actions to address systemic issues, and continuously monitoring and reviewing service performance to identify potential risks and opportunities for improvement. By taking a proactive approach to SLA management, organizations can reduce the likelihood of future violations and enhance service delivery capabilities.

cssCopy code

```
$           implement_proactive_measures        --
conduct_root_cause_analysis                      --
implement_corrective_actions                     --
monitor_service_performance
```

Documentation is essential for documenting SLA violations, actions taken to address them, and lessons learned for future reference. Organizations should maintain comprehensive records of SLA violations, including details such as the nature of the violation, impact on service delivery, actions taken to resolve the issue, and any follow-up measures implemented to prevent recurrence. By documenting SLA violations and associated actions, organizations can track trends over time, identify recurring issues, and implement preventive measures to mitigate risks and improve service quality.

cssCopy code

```
$ maintain_documentation --record_SLA_violations --
document_actions_taken --track_trends
```

Regular review and analysis of SLA performance data are essential for identifying trends, patterns, and areas for improvement. Organizations should conduct periodic reviews of SLA performance metrics, compare actual performance against agreed-upon targets, and identify any deviations or trends that may indicate potential issues or opportunities for improvement. By analyzing SLA performance data regularly, organizations can proactively identify and address emerging issues, optimize service delivery processes, and enhance overall service quality.

cssCopy code

```
$ conduct_periodic_reviews --compare_performance --identify_deviation --analyze_trends
```

In summary, protocols for handling SLA violations are essential for maintaining service quality, managing customer expectations, and preserving organizational reputation. By establishing clear protocols, defining escalation procedures, communicating effectively with stakeholders, implementing proactive measures, documenting SLA violations, and analyzing performance data regularly, organizations can effectively manage SLA violations, minimize their impact on service delivery, and drive continuous improvement in service quality and customer satisfaction. Effective SLA violation management requires collaboration, transparency, and a proactive approach to addressing issues and improving service delivery capabilities.

Escalation procedures for resolving SLA breaches are vital components of service level agreement (SLA) management, providing structured pathways for addressing issues and restoring service delivery to acceptable levels. When SLA breaches occur, it's crucial for organizations to respond swiftly and effectively, escalating the matter through predefined channels to ensure timely resolution and minimize the impact on service quality and customer satisfaction. By establishing clear escalation procedures, defining escalation paths, and empowering designated personnel to take appropriate actions, organizations can effectively manage SLA breaches and uphold their commitments to customers and stakeholders.

To initiate the escalation process, organizations must first establish clear escalation procedures that outline the steps to be followed when an SLA breach occurs. This involves defining the criteria for identifying an SLA breach, such as exceeding predefined thresholds for response or resolution times, downtime exceeding agreed-upon limits, or failure to meet service availability targets. By clearly defining these criteria, organizations can ensure consistency in identifying and responding to SLA breaches across different service offerings and customer engagements.

cssCopy code

```
$ establish_escalation_procedures --define_criteria --identify_SLA_breaches
```

Once an SLA breach is identified, organizations must initiate the escalation process by following predefined escalation paths. These paths typically involve escalating the issue through a hierarchy of personnel or teams, starting from frontline support staff and escalating to higher levels of management or specialized teams as necessary. By establishing clear escalation paths, organizations can ensure that SLA breaches are addressed promptly and effectively, with issues being escalated to the appropriate level of expertise and authority for resolution.

cssCopy code

```
$  initiate_escalation  --follow_escalation_paths  --escalate_to_higher_authorities
```

Designated personnel responsible for managing SLA breaches should be empowered to take appropriate actions to address the issue and restore service delivery to acceptable levels. This may involve deploying additional resources, engaging specialized teams or vendors, or implementing temporary workarounds to mitigate the impact of the breach on service quality and customer satisfaction. By empowering designated personnel to take decisive action, organizations can expedite the resolution process and minimize the negative consequences of SLA breaches.

cssCopy code

```
$        empower_designated_personnel        --deploy_additional_resources        --engage_specialized_teams --implement_workarounds
```

Effective communication is essential during the escalation process to ensure that all relevant stakeholders are kept informed of the situation and its resolution status. This may involve notifying affected customers or clients of the SLA breach, providing regular updates on the progress of remediation efforts, and offering assurances and remedies to mitigate the impact on service delivery. By maintaining open and transparent communication channels, organizations can build trust with stakeholders and demonstrate their commitment to resolving SLA breaches promptly and effectively.

cssCopy code

```
$           communicate_effectively           --
notify_affected_stakeholders           --
provide_regular_updates --offer_assurances
```

In addition to addressing SLA breaches reactively, organizations should also implement proactive measures to prevent future breaches and improve overall service quality. This may involve conducting root cause analysis to identify underlying issues contributing to SLA breaches, implementing corrective actions to address systemic issues, and continuously monitoring and reviewing service performance to identify potential risks and opportunities for improvement. By taking a proactive approach to SLA management, organizations can reduce the likelihood of future breaches and enhance their ability to deliver high-quality services consistently.

cssCopy code

```
$           implement_proactive_measures           --
conduct_root_cause_analysis           --
implement_corrective_actions           --
monitor_service_performance
```

Documentation is essential for documenting SLA breaches, actions taken to address them, and lessons learned for future reference. Organizations should maintain comprehensive records of SLA breaches, including details such as the nature of the breach, impact on service delivery, actions taken to resolve the issue, and any follow-up measures implemented to prevent recurrence. By documenting SLA breaches and associated actions, organizations can track trends over time, identify recurring issues, and implement preventive measures to mitigate risks and improve service quality.

cssCopy code

```
$ maintain_documentation --record_SLA_breaches --document_actions_taken --track_trends
```

In summary, escalation procedures are critical for resolving SLA breaches promptly and effectively, minimizing their impact on service delivery and customer satisfaction. By establishing clear escalation procedures, defining escalation paths, empowering designated personnel to take appropriate actions, communicating effectively with stakeholders, implementing proactive measures, and maintaining comprehensive documentation, organizations can effectively manage SLA breaches and uphold their commitments to customers and stakeholders. Effective SLA breach management requires collaboration, transparency, and a proactive approach to addressing issues and improving service delivery capabilities.

Chapter 6: Continuous Improvement of SLAs

Regular review and revision of service level agreements (SLAs) are essential aspects of effective service management, ensuring that SLAs remain aligned with evolving business needs, technology trends, and customer expectations. As organizations strive to deliver high-quality services and meet changing demands, it's imperative to periodically evaluate and adjust SLAs to reflect current priorities, performance targets, and service offerings. By establishing a systematic process for reviewing and revising SLAs, organizations can optimize service delivery, enhance customer satisfaction, and drive continuous improvement across their operations.

To initiate the review and revision process, organizations must first establish clear guidelines and timelines for conducting SLA reviews. This involves defining the frequency of reviews, specifying the stakeholders involved, and outlining the criteria for assessing SLA effectiveness and relevance. By setting clear expectations and timelines for SLA reviews, organizations can ensure that these critical assessments are conducted regularly and systematically, without undue delay or oversight.

```css
cssCopy code
$ establish_review_guidelines --define_review_frequency
--specify_stakeholders --outline_criteria
```

During the review process, organizations should assess the performance of existing SLAs against predefined metrics and targets, identifying areas of strength and opportunities for improvement. This may involve analyzing historical performance data, soliciting feedback from stakeholders, and benchmarking against industry standards and best practices. By conducting comprehensive evaluations of SLA performance, organizations can identify gaps, inefficiencies, and emerging trends that may necessitate revisions to existing SLAs.

cssCopy code

```
$ assess_SLA_performance --analyze_performance_data --solicit_stakeholder_feedback --benchmark_against_standards
```

In addition to evaluating performance metrics, organizations should also consider changes in business requirements, market dynamics, and regulatory environments that may impact SLA effectiveness and relevance. This may involve assessing shifts in customer preferences, technological advancements, or competitive pressures that could influence service delivery priorities and performance expectations. By staying attuned to external factors and emerging trends, organizations can proactively adapt their SLAs to address evolving needs and challenges.

cssCopy code

```
$ consider_business_requirements --assess_market_dynamics --evaluate_regulatory_changes
```

Stakeholder engagement is critical throughout the review and revision process, ensuring that SLAs reflect the collective input and priorities of all relevant parties. This may involve convening regular meetings or workshops with key stakeholders, including business leaders, service owners, and end users, to solicit feedback, discuss performance issues, and prioritize revisions. By fostering open dialogue and collaboration, organizations can ensure that SLAs are aligned with stakeholder expectations and strategic objectives.

cssCopy code

```
$    engage_stakeholders    --conduct_meetings    --solicit_feedback --prioritize_revisions
```

Once areas for improvement have been identified and priorities established, organizations can proceed with revising existing SLAs or developing new ones to address evolving needs and objectives. This may involve updating performance targets, refining service scope and definitions, or incorporating new service offerings or technologies into SLA commitments. By iteratively refining SLAs based on feedback and insights gained from the review process, organizations can enhance their ability to meet customer expectations and deliver value-added services.

cssCopy code

```
$ revise_existing_SLAs --update_performance_targets --refine_service_scope --incorporate_new_technologies
```

Following the revision of SLAs, organizations should communicate changes to all relevant stakeholders and ensure that updated SLAs are properly documented and disseminated. This may involve distributing revised SLAs to affected parties, providing training or guidance on updated performance metrics and expectations, and updating internal documentation and systems to reflect changes. By maintaining transparency and clarity throughout the revision process, organizations can minimize confusion and ensure that stakeholders are informed and aligned with revised SLA commitments.

cssCopy code

```
$  communicate_changes  --distribute_revised_SLAs  --
provide_training --update_documentation
```

Continuous monitoring and evaluation are essential to ensure that revised SLAs remain effective and relevant over time. Organizations should establish mechanisms for ongoing performance monitoring, feedback collection, and periodic reviews to assess the impact of revised SLAs and identify areas for further refinement. By adopting a cyclical approach to SLA management, organizations can continuously adapt and improve their service delivery capabilities, maintaining alignment with evolving business needs and customer expectations.

cssCopy code

```
$   monitor_performance    --collect_feedback    --
conduct_periodic_reviews                          --
identify_areas_for_refinement
```

In summary, regular review and revision of SLAs are essential for maintaining alignment with business objectives, technology trends, and customer expectations. By establishing systematic processes for SLA review, engaging stakeholders throughout the process, and incorporating feedback and insights into SLA revisions, organizations can optimize service delivery, enhance customer satisfaction, and drive continuous improvement across their operations. Effective SLA management requires proactive engagement, transparency, and a commitment to adaptability and continuous improvement to meet evolving needs and challenges.

Incorporating feedback for SLA enhancement is a crucial aspect of service desk management, ensuring that service level agreements (SLAs) remain aligned with evolving business needs and customer expectations. Feedback serves as a valuable source of insight, providing organizations with actionable data and perspectives to identify areas for improvement, refine performance metrics, and enhance service delivery capabilities. By systematically collecting, analyzing, and incorporating feedback into SLA refinement processes, organizations can optimize service quality, strengthen customer relationships, and drive continuous improvement across their operations.

To initiate the feedback collection process, organizations must establish mechanisms for soliciting input from all relevant stakeholders, including customers, internal teams, and business partners. This may involve deploying surveys, conducting focus groups, or leveraging feedback management platforms to gather insights on service performance, user satisfaction, and areas for improvement. By leveraging these feedback channels, organizations can capture diverse perspectives and actionable insights to inform SLA enhancement efforts.

Once feedback has been collected, organizations must systematically analyze and prioritize input to identify actionable insights and areas for improvement. This may involve aggregating feedback data, categorizing input based on themes or trends, and conducting root cause analysis to understand underlying issues impacting service performance. By leveraging analytical tools and techniques, organizations can distill feedback into actionable insights and prioritize enhancement opportunities based on their potential impact on service quality and customer satisfaction.

Following the analysis phase, organizations must collaborate with stakeholders to develop actionable plans for incorporating feedback into SLA enhancement efforts. This may involve convening cross-functional teams to review feedback findings, identify improvement initiatives, and develop action plans for implementing changes. By fostering collaboration and buy-in across the organization, organizations can ensure that feedback-driven enhancements are aligned with strategic objectives and operational priorities.

Once enhancement initiatives have been identified, organizations must execute action plans and monitor their impact on service performance and customer satisfaction. This may involve deploying new processes, updating performance metrics, or refining service delivery practices based on feedback-driven insights. By systematically implementing feedback-driven enhancements and monitoring their impact over time, organizations can validate the effectiveness of their improvement efforts and make iterative adjustments as needed.

In addition to implementing feedback-driven enhancements, organizations must also communicate changes to stakeholders and ensure that updated SLAs reflect the incorporation of feedback. This may involve updating SLA documentation, communicating revised performance metrics and targets to relevant parties, and providing training or guidance on new service delivery practices. By maintaining transparency and clarity throughout the enhancement process, organizations can ensure that stakeholders are informed and aligned with the changes being made to SLAs.

Continuous monitoring and evaluation are essential to ensure that feedback-driven enhancements deliver the intended benefits and address identified areas for improvement. Organizations must establish mechanisms for ongoing performance monitoring, feedback collection, and periodic reviews to assess the impact of enhancement initiatives and identify further refinement opportunities. By adopting a cyclical approach to SLA enhancement, organizations can continuously adapt and improve their service delivery capabilities, maintaining alignment with evolving business needs and customer expectations.

In summary, incorporating feedback for SLA enhancement is a critical practice for optimizing service quality, strengthening customer relationships, and driving continuous improvement in service desk management. By systematically collecting, analyzing, and incorporating feedback into SLA refinement processes, organizations can identify areas for improvement, refine performance metrics, and enhance service delivery capabilities to meet evolving business needs and customer expectations. Effective feedback integration requires proactive engagement, collaboration, and a commitment to continuous improvement to drive meaningful enhancements in service quality and customer satisfaction.

Chapter 7: SLA Automation and Tools

Implementing automated SLA management systems is pivotal in modern service desk operations, offering organizations a streamlined approach to monitoring, enforcing, and optimizing service level agreements (SLAs) to ensure consistent service delivery and adherence to contractual obligations. Automated SLA management systems leverage advanced technologies, such as service desk software platforms and integrated monitoring tools, to automate key aspects of SLA management, including SLA tracking, performance measurement, and escalation management. By deploying these systems, organizations can enhance operational efficiency, improve service quality, and mitigate the risk of SLA breaches, thereby fostering stronger customer relationships and driving business success.

To initiate the implementation process, organizations must first select a suitable automated SLA management system that aligns with their unique requirements, operational processes, and technology infrastructure. This may involve conducting a thorough assessment of available solutions, evaluating features and functionalities, and selecting a vendor that offers a comprehensive solution tailored to the organization's needs. Once a system has been chosen, organizations can proceed with the deployment process, which typically involves several key steps.

One essential step in implementing automated SLA management systems is configuring SLA parameters and performance metrics within the system to align with organizational objectives and customer requirements. This may involve defining SLA categories, setting performance targets, and establishing escalation rules based on predefined criteria. By customizing SLA parameters to reflect specific service offerings and customer expectations, organizations can ensure that the automated system accurately monitors and measures service performance against agreed-upon standards.

After configuring SLA parameters, organizations must integrate the automated SLA management system with existing service desk tools, systems, and processes to enable seamless data exchange and workflow automation. This may involve integrating the SLA management system with ticketing systems, monitoring tools, and customer relationship management (CRM) platforms to facilitate real-time data synchronization and automated incident tracking. By integrating disparate systems and automating data exchange, organizations can streamline SLA management workflows, minimize manual intervention, and improve data accuracy and consistency.

Once the automated SLA management system has been configured and integrated, organizations must conduct thorough testing and validation to ensure that the system operates as intended and meets performance requirements. This may involve conducting user acceptance testing (UAT) to validate system functionality, performance testing to assess system scalability and responsiveness, and data validation to verify the accuracy and reliability of SLA tracking and reporting capabilities. By rigorously testing the system before deployment, organizations can identify and address any issues or discrepancies to ensure a smooth and successful implementation.

Following testing and validation, organizations can proceed with the rollout of the automated SLA management system across the organization, which may involve training end-users, administrators, and support staff on system functionality, best practices, and SLA management procedures. This may include providing hands-on training sessions, user documentation, and online resources to educate stakeholders on how to effectively use the system to monitor, track, and manage SLAs. By empowering users with the knowledge and skills to leverage the automated SLA management system effectively, organizations can maximize the system's value and drive widespread adoption across the organization.

Once the automated SLA management system is deployed, organizations must establish ongoing monitoring, maintenance, and governance processes to ensure the continued effectiveness and reliability of the system. This may involve conducting regular system audits to identify areas for optimization, implementing software updates and patches to address security vulnerabilities and performance issues, and reviewing SLA performance data to identify trends, patterns, and areas for improvement. By proactively managing and maintaining the automated SLA management system, organizations can ensure that it remains aligned with evolving business needs and continues to deliver value over time.

In summary, implementing automated SLA management systems is essential for modern service desk operations, enabling organizations to streamline SLA management processes, improve service quality, and enhance customer satisfaction. By configuring, integrating, testing, and deploying automated SLA management systems effectively, organizations can automate key aspects of SLA monitoring and enforcement, minimize manual effort, and optimize service delivery workflows. With proper training, ongoing monitoring, and maintenance, organizations can maximize the value of automated SLA management systems, driving operational efficiency, and achieving business objectives.

Utilizing tools for SLA monitoring and enforcement is crucial for modern service desk operations, empowering organizations to effectively track, measure, and enforce service level agreements (SLAs) to ensure optimal service delivery and adherence to contractual commitments. These tools encompass a range of technologies and platforms designed to automate key aspects of SLA management, including SLA tracking, performance monitoring, and escalation management, thereby enabling organizations to proactively identify and address potential service disruptions and minimize the risk of SLA breaches. By leveraging these tools, organizations can enhance operational efficiency, improve service quality, and enhance customer satisfaction.

One of the primary tools for SLA monitoring and enforcement is service desk software, which provides a centralized platform for managing service requests, incidents, and SLAs. Popular service desk software solutions include ServiceNow, Jira Service Desk, and Zendesk, among others. These platforms offer features such as SLA tracking, ticket prioritization, and automated workflows, enabling organizations to streamline service desk operations and ensure timely resolution of customer issues. Using service desk software, organizations can define SLA parameters, set performance targets, and monitor SLA compliance in real-time, allowing them to proactively identify and address potential SLA breaches before they occur.

In addition to service desk software, organizations can leverage monitoring and alerting tools to track service performance and identify potential issues that may impact SLA compliance. Tools such as Nagios, Zabbix, and SolarWinds Network Performance Monitor enable organizations to monitor key performance indicators (KPIs) such as network uptime, server availability, and application performance in real-time. By configuring these tools to monitor SLA-related metrics, organizations can receive alerts and notifications when performance thresholds are exceeded, allowing them to take corrective action and mitigate the risk of SLA breaches.

Another essential tool for SLA monitoring and enforcement is reporting and analytics software, which enables organizations to generate comprehensive reports and dashboards to track SLA performance and identify trends and patterns over time. Tools such as Tableau, Power BI, and Splunk allow organizations to visualize SLA performance data, analyze trends, and identify areas for improvement. By leveraging reporting and analytics software, organizations can gain actionable insights into their SLA performance, identify root causes of SLA breaches, and make data-driven decisions to optimize service delivery and enhance customer satisfaction.

In addition to these tools, organizations can also utilize ticketing and workflow automation tools to streamline SLA management processes and ensure consistent enforcement of SLA commitments. Tools such as Jira, Asana, and Trello enable organizations to automate ticket routing, prioritize tasks, and enforce SLA-related workflows, reducing manual effort and minimizing the risk of human error. By automating routine tasks and workflows, organizations can improve operational efficiency, reduce response times, and enhance overall service desk performance.

To deploy these tools effectively, organizations must first assess their SLA monitoring and enforcement requirements and select tools that align with their unique needs, objectives, and technology infrastructure. Once selected, organizations can configure and customize the tools to meet their specific SLA management requirements, including defining SLA parameters, setting performance targets, and configuring alerting and notification rules. Additionally, organizations should provide comprehensive training and support to end-users and administrators to ensure they understand how to effectively use the tools to monitor, track, and enforce SLAs.

By leveraging tools for SLA monitoring and enforcement, organizations can effectively manage SLA commitments, optimize service delivery processes, and enhance customer satisfaction. These tools enable organizations to automate key aspects of SLA management, streamline service desk operations, and ensure consistent enforcement of SLA commitments, thereby enabling organizations to meet their service level objectives and drive business success.

Chapter 8: SLA Governance and Compliance

Establishing governance frameworks for SLA management is paramount for organizations seeking to ensure the effective implementation, monitoring, and enforcement of service level agreements (SLAs). A governance framework provides the structure, policies, procedures, and accountability mechanisms necessary to govern SLA-related activities and ensure alignment with organizational goals, objectives, and regulatory requirements. By establishing robust governance frameworks, organizations can enhance transparency, accountability, and compliance, thereby mitigating risks, optimizing service delivery, and fostering trust and confidence among stakeholders.

One essential aspect of establishing governance frameworks for SLA management is defining clear roles and responsibilities for all stakeholders involved in the SLA lifecycle. This includes delineating the responsibilities of service desk managers, IT service providers, customers, and other relevant parties in defining, implementing, and monitoring SLAs. By clearly defining roles and responsibilities, organizations can ensure accountability and ownership for SLA-related activities, facilitating effective collaboration and communication among stakeholders.

To deploy a governance framework for SLA management, organizations can utilize IT service management (ITSM) frameworks such as ITIL

(Information Technology Infrastructure Library) or COBIT (Control Objectives for Information and Related Technologies). These frameworks provide guidance and best practices for establishing governance structures, processes, and controls for IT service delivery, including SLA management. For example, ITIL offers guidance on defining service level agreements, negotiating SLAs with customers, and monitoring and reporting SLA performance.

In addition to leveraging ITSM frameworks, organizations can also establish SLA governance committees or steering groups tasked with overseeing SLA-related activities and ensuring alignment with organizational objectives. These committees typically include representatives from various stakeholders, including IT, business units, legal, and compliance teams, and are responsible for defining SLA policies, approving SLA templates, and resolving disputes or escalations related to SLA performance.

An important aspect of SLA governance is establishing clear SLA policies and standards that govern the creation, negotiation, and management of SLAs across the organization. These policies should define the criteria for determining which services are eligible for SLAs, the process for negotiating SLAs with customers, and the metrics and targets used to measure SLA performance. By establishing clear policies and standards, organizations can ensure consistency and standardization in SLA management practices, reducing ambiguity and confusion among stakeholders.

To enforce SLA governance, organizations can implement SLA management tools and systems that automate key aspects of SLA management, including SLA tracking, performance monitoring, and reporting. These tools enable organizations to define SLA parameters, track SLA performance in real-time, and generate comprehensive reports and dashboards to monitor SLA compliance. Popular SLA management tools include ServiceNow, BMC Remedy, and SolarWinds Service Desk, among others.

Another critical aspect of SLA governance is establishing robust processes and controls for managing changes to SLAs. This includes defining change management procedures for requesting, reviewing, and approving changes to SLA metrics, targets, or terms. Organizations can utilize change management tools such as Jira, ServiceNow Change Management, or Microsoft Azure DevOps to automate and streamline the change management process and ensure that changes to SLAs are implemented in a controlled and compliant manner.

Furthermore, organizations should implement regular SLA reviews and audits to assess SLA performance, identify areas for improvement, and address any non-compliance issues. These reviews should involve stakeholders from both the IT and business sides of the organization and should include an assessment of SLA metrics, targets, and performance against agreed-upon standards. By conducting regular reviews and audits, organizations can identify trends, patterns, and opportunities for optimization, enabling continuous improvement in SLA management practices.

In summary, establishing governance frameworks for SLA management is essential for organizations seeking to optimize service delivery, mitigate risks, and enhance customer satisfaction. By defining clear roles and responsibilities, leveraging ITSM frameworks, establishing SLA policies and standards, implementing SLA management tools, and conducting regular reviews and audits, organizations can ensure effective governance of SLAs and drive business success.

Ensuring compliance with legal and regulatory requirements is a critical aspect of managing service desk operations in any organization. In today's complex regulatory landscape, organizations must navigate various laws, regulations, and industry standards to protect sensitive data, mitigate risks, and maintain trust with customers and stakeholders. Failure to comply with these requirements can result in severe consequences, including financial penalties, legal liabilities, and reputational damage. Therefore, it is essential for organizations to establish robust compliance programs and implement effective mechanisms to ensure adherence to applicable laws and regulations.

One of the fundamental steps in ensuring compliance is conducting a thorough assessment of relevant legal and regulatory requirements that apply to the organization's operations. This involves identifying applicable laws, regulations, industry standards, and contractual obligations that govern the organization's activities, particularly those related to data protection, privacy, security, and confidentiality. For example, organizations operating in the healthcare sector must comply with the Health Insurance Portability and Accountability Act (HIPAA), while those in the financial services industry must adhere to regulations such as the Sarbanes-Oxley Act (SOX) and the Payment Card Industry Data Security Standard (PCI DSS).

Once the applicable legal and regulatory requirements have been identified, organizations must establish policies, procedures, and controls to ensure compliance with these requirements. This may include implementing data protection measures such as encryption, access controls, and data masking to safeguard sensitive information, as well as establishing protocols for handling and disposing of data in accordance with legal and regulatory requirements. For example, organizations subject to the European Union's General Data Protection Regulation (GDPR) must implement measures to ensure the lawful processing of personal data, including obtaining explicit consent from data subjects and providing mechanisms for data subjects to exercise their rights under the GDPR.

In addition to implementing technical controls, organizations must also invest in training and awareness programs to educate employees about their obligations and responsibilities regarding legal and regulatory compliance. This includes providing training on data privacy and security best practices, raising awareness about potential risks and vulnerabilities, and empowering employees to report any suspected violations or breaches of compliance requirements.

Furthermore, organizations should designate compliance officers or teams responsible for overseeing compliance efforts, monitoring regulatory developments, and ensuring that policies and procedures are up to date and effective.

To deploy technical controls and enforce compliance, organizations can leverage various tools and technologies designed to help manage and monitor regulatory compliance. For example, configuration management tools such as Ansible or Puppet can be used to automate the deployment and enforcement of security configurations and policies across IT infrastructure. Similarly, vulnerability management tools such as Nessus or Qualys can help identify and remediate security vulnerabilities that may pose compliance risks. Additionally, organizations can utilize compliance management software solutions that provide centralized visibility into compliance status, automate compliance assessments, and generate audit reports to demonstrate adherence to regulatory requirements.

Furthermore, organizations should conduct regular audits and assessments to evaluate their compliance posture and identify any gaps or areas for improvement. This may involve internal audits conducted by internal audit teams or external audits conducted by independent third-party auditors or regulatory authorities. Audits typically involve reviewing documentation, interviewing personnel, and performing technical assessments to assess compliance with applicable laws, regulations, and industry standards.

Organizations should promptly address any findings or recommendations resulting from audits and take corrective action to mitigate compliance risks and improve their overall compliance posture.

In summary, ensuring compliance with legal and regulatory requirements is a multifaceted endeavor that requires a proactive and comprehensive approach. By identifying applicable requirements, establishing policies and procedures, implementing technical controls, providing training and awareness, and conducting regular audits and assessments, organizations can effectively mitigate compliance risks and demonstrate their commitment to upholding legal and regulatory standards. Compliance should be viewed not only as a legal obligation but also as a strategic imperative that contributes to organizational resilience, trust, and reputation in the marketplace.

Chapter 9: Advanced SLA Negotiation Techniques

Advanced negotiation strategies are essential when dealing with complex Service Level Agreement (SLA) agreements, particularly in situations where multiple stakeholders, diverse interests, and intricate requirements must be carefully navigated to achieve mutually beneficial outcomes. In such scenarios, traditional negotiation approaches may not suffice, requiring sophisticated strategies and tactics to address the complexities involved.

One advanced negotiation strategy is to conduct a thorough analysis of the parties involved, their interests, priorities, and potential areas of compromise. This involves gathering information about the stakeholders' objectives, concerns, and constraints, as well as assessing their bargaining power and leverage in the negotiation process. By understanding the interests and motivations of all parties, negotiators can tailor their approach to accommodate diverse perspectives and foster collaborative problem-solving.

Another effective strategy is to employ a principled negotiation approach, as advocated by the Harvard Negotiation Project. This approach focuses on separating the people from the problem, focusing on interests rather than positions, generating options for mutual gain, and insisting on objective criteria for agreement. By adopting a principled negotiation approach, negotiators can create value, build trust, and reach agreements that meet the needs of all parties involved.

Furthermore, leveraging technology can enhance the negotiation process and facilitate collaboration among stakeholders. For instance, using collaborative negotiation platforms or project management tools such as Asana or Trello can streamline communication, document sharing, and decision-making, enabling stakeholders to work together more effectively and efficiently. Additionally, virtual negotiation tools such as Zoom or Microsoft Teams can facilitate remote negotiations, allowing parties to engage in real-time discussions and negotiations from anywhere in the world.

In complex SLA negotiations, it is crucial to establish clear objectives and priorities upfront and to maintain flexibility and adaptability throughout the negotiation process. This involves identifying the critical issues that require resolution, prioritizing them based on their importance and impact, and developing strategies to address them effectively. Negotiators should also anticipate potential challenges and obstacles and develop contingency plans to overcome them.

Moreover, building relationships and fostering trust among stakeholders is essential for successful negotiation outcomes. This involves investing time and effort in building rapport, understanding each other's perspectives, and demonstrating a commitment to collaboration and mutual respect. By establishing trust and rapport, negotiators can create a positive negotiation environment conducive to constructive dialogue and problem-solving.

Additionally, employing creative problem-solving techniques can help break deadlocks and overcome impasses in complex SLA negotiations. This may involve brainstorming alternative solutions, exploring trade-offs and concessions, or introducing innovative approaches to address conflicting interests and reconcile differences. By thinking outside the box and considering novel solutions, negotiators can unlock value and achieve outcomes that may not have been apparent initially.

Furthermore, incorporating objective criteria and benchmarks into the negotiation process can help ensure fairness, transparency, and accountability. This involves establishing clear metrics, standards, and benchmarks against which the performance of the SLA agreement can be evaluated objectively. By anchoring the negotiation discussions around objective criteria, negotiators can depersonalize the negotiation process and focus on finding solutions that meet the specified criteria and standards.

Lastly, it is essential to maintain open lines of communication and to actively manage expectations throughout the negotiation process. This involves providing regular updates, seeking feedback, and addressing concerns and questions promptly and transparently. By keeping stakeholders informed and engaged, negotiators can build consensus, manage conflicts, and facilitate agreement on complex SLA agreements.

In summary, advanced negotiation strategies are essential for navigating complex SLA agreements effectively. By conducting thorough analyses, employing principled negotiation approaches, leveraging technology, establishing clear objectives, building relationships, fostering trust, employing creative problem-solving techniques, incorporating objective criteria, and maintaining open communication, negotiators can achieve successful outcomes and create value for all parties involved in the negotiation process. Resolving disputes and conflicts is a critical aspect of SLA negotiations, ensuring that parties can reach mutually acceptable agreements and uphold the integrity of the service level agreements. When conflicts arise during negotiations, it's essential to address them promptly and effectively to prevent them from escalating further and jeopardizing the negotiation process. One technique for resolving disputes is to employ a collaborative problem-solving approach, where parties work together to identify underlying issues, explore potential solutions, and reach consensus. This approach emphasizes communication, empathy, and cooperation, fostering a constructive atmosphere conducive to resolving conflicts amicably. To deploy this technique, negotiators can use mediation or facilitated negotiation sessions to facilitate dialogue and promote understanding between conflicting parties. Additionally, employing active listening techniques, such as paraphrasing and summarizing, can help ensure that all parties feel heard and understood, facilitating the resolution of disputes. Moreover, when conflicts arise due to differing interpretations of SLA terms or performance metrics, it's essential to refer to objective criteria and benchmarks to guide the resolution process. By anchoring discussions around objective standards, negotiators can depersonalize conflicts and focus on finding solutions that align with the agreed-upon criteria. For example, if there is a dispute over whether a service level has been met, parties can refer to historical performance data or industry benchmarks to assess performance objectively and resolve the dispute. Furthermore, involving neutral third parties, such as mediators or subject matter experts, can help facilitate the resolution of complex disputes by providing unbiased perspectives and guiding parties towards mutually beneficial solutions. These third parties can offer insights, expertise, and alternative viewpoints that may help parties overcome impasses and find common ground. To engage third parties effectively, negotiators can use platforms like Zoom or Microsoft Teams to facilitate virtual mediation sessions or expert consultations. Additionally, when conflicts arise due to differences in expectations or priorities, it's crucial to engage in principled negotiation techniques, focusing on interests rather than positions and generating options for mutual gain. By exploring creative solutions and trade-offs, parties can often find win-win outcomes that address underlying concerns and satisfy the needs of all parties involved. For instance, if there is a disagreement over service delivery timelines, parties can explore alternative scheduling options or resource allocations to meet the needs of both parties. Furthermore, establishing clear escalation procedures and dispute resolution mechanisms in the SLA can help prevent conflicts from escalating and provide a framework for addressing disputes as they arise. These procedures should outline the steps for escalating disputes to higher levels of management or engaging in formal arbitration or mediation processes if necessary. By establishing clear procedures upfront, parties can streamline the resolution process and ensure that disputes are addressed promptly and effectively. Additionally, maintaining open lines of communication throughout the negotiation process is essential for identifying and addressing conflicts early on. Parties should feel comfortable expressing their concerns and grievances and should be encouraged to collaborate openly to find mutually acceptable solutions. By fostering a culture of transparency and cooperation, negotiators can mitigate the risk of conflicts arising and promote positive outcomes in SLA negotiations. In summary, resolving disputes and conflicts is a critical aspect of SLA negotiations, requiring effective communication, collaboration, and problem-solving skills. By employing collaborative problem-solving approaches, referring to objective criteria and benchmarks, engaging neutral third parties, using principled negotiation techniques, establishing clear escalation procedures, and maintaining open communication, parties can navigate conflicts effectively and reach mutually beneficial agreements in SLA negotiations.

Chapter 10: Case Studies: Effective SLA Management in Service Desk Operations

Real-world examples of successful SLA implementation and management provide invaluable insights into how organizations leverage SLAs to enhance service delivery, drive performance improvements, and strengthen customer relationships. One prominent example is the service level agreement between Amazon Web Services (AWS) and its customers. AWS offers a comprehensive set of cloud computing services, including storage, computing power, and networking, to businesses worldwide. Their SLAs guarantee specific levels of service availability, performance, and support responsiveness, providing customers with confidence in the reliability and performance of AWS services.

To deploy this technique, AWS utilizes a combination of monitoring tools and automated alerts to track service performance in real-time. For instance, AWS CloudWatch enables customers to monitor their cloud resources and applications, collect and analyze log data, and set up alarms to notify them of any deviations from predefined performance thresholds. By proactively monitoring service metrics, AWS can identify potential issues before they impact customers and take corrective actions to maintain service availability and performance. Additionally, AWS provides customers with a dashboard that displays key performance metrics and SLA compliance status, enabling them to track service performance and ensure compliance with SLA commitments.

Another example of successful SLA implementation and management is the partnership between a managed IT services provider and a healthcare organization. The IT services provider offers a range of IT support services, including network monitoring, help desk support, and cybersecurity services, to the healthcare organization. Their SLA defines specific service levels for response times, issue resolution, and system availability, tailored to the healthcare organization's unique needs and priorities.

To deploy this technique, the IT services provider leverages a combination of monitoring tools, ticketing systems, and escalation procedures to manage service delivery and ensure SLA compliance. For example, they use network monitoring tools to proactively identify and address potential issues, ticketing systems to track and prioritize customer requests, and escalation procedures to escalate critical issues to senior engineers or management for resolution. By adhering to SLA commitments and maintaining high levels of service quality, the IT services provider helps the healthcare organization improve operational efficiency, minimize downtime, and deliver better patient care.

Furthermore, telecommunications companies often employ SLAs to guarantee service reliability and performance for their customers. For instance, a mobile network operator may offer SLAs that define specific performance metrics for network availability, call quality, and data speeds. To ensure compliance with these SLAs, the mobile network operator deploys a variety of techniques, including network monitoring, performance testing, and capacity planning.

To deploy this technique, the mobile network operator utilizes network monitoring tools to continuously monitor the performance of its infrastructure, identify potential bottlenecks or issues, and optimize network resources to meet service level commitments. Additionally, they conduct regular performance testing to assess network performance under different conditions and ensure that it meets or exceeds SLA requirements. Capacity planning is also crucial, as it allows the mobile network operator to anticipate future demand and scale their infrastructure accordingly to maintain service quality and meet SLA commitments.

In summary, real-world examples of successful SLA implementation and management demonstrate the importance of proactive monitoring, effective communication, and continuous improvement in ensuring service quality and meeting customer expectations. By leveraging monitoring tools, ticketing systems, escalation procedures, and capacity planning techniques, organizations can optimize service delivery, minimize downtime, and build trust and loyalty with their customers through SLA compliance.

Lessons learned and best practices gleaned from case studies provide invaluable insights into the intricacies of real-world scenarios, offering a rich tapestry of experiences from which organizations can draw inspiration and guidance for their own endeavors. One such case study revolves around the adoption of Agile methodologies by a software development company. In this case, the company transitioned from traditional waterfall development to Agile practices, aiming to improve collaboration, responsiveness, and product quality.

To initiate this transition, the company conducted extensive training sessions to familiarize teams with Agile principles and practices. They introduced tools such as Jira and Trello to facilitate Agile project management, enabling teams to plan sprints, track progress, and manage backlogs effectively. By embracing Agile, the company achieved greater flexibility in responding to changing customer needs, reduced time-to-market for new features, and enhanced overall product quality.

Another case study pertains to the implementation of DevOps practices by a large e-commerce platform. Facing challenges with frequent software releases and operational silos, the company embarked on a DevOps transformation journey to streamline collaboration between development and operations teams, automate deployment processes, and improve system reliability.

To facilitate this transformation, the company adopted tools such as Jenkins for continuous integration and deployment, Docker for containerization, and Kubernetes for orchestration. They also implemented infrastructure as code principles using tools like Terraform and Ansible to automate infrastructure provisioning and configuration management. Through this initiative, the company achieved faster release cycles, reduced deployment failures, and increased system stability, resulting in improved customer satisfaction and business outcomes.

Moreover, a case study centered on the digital transformation of a financial institution highlights the importance of organizational change management in driving successful initiatives. Faced with evolving customer expectations and increasing competition from fintech startups, the institution embarked on a journey to modernize its legacy systems, enhance digital capabilities, and improve customer experiences.

To navigate this transformation, the institution established a dedicated change management team tasked with fostering a culture of innovation, collaboration, and continuous improvement across the organization. They conducted regular communication sessions, training workshops, and feedback sessions to engage employees and address concerns throughout the transformation process. Additionally, they leveraged tools such as Slack and Microsoft Teams to facilitate communication and collaboration among distributed teams.

As a result of these efforts, the financial institution successfully launched new digital products and services, streamlined internal processes, and improved customer satisfaction metrics. By embracing change management principles and fostering a culture of innovation, the institution positioned itself for long-term success in a rapidly evolving market.

Furthermore, a case study involving a healthcare organization underscores the importance of resilience and adaptability in navigating unforeseen challenges. Faced with the COVID-19 pandemic, the organization had to rapidly adjust its operations to accommodate remote work arrangements, ensure patient safety, and maintain continuity of care.

To address these challenges, the organization implemented telehealth solutions to enable virtual consultations and remote monitoring of patients. They also deployed collaboration tools such as Zoom and Microsoft Teams to facilitate communication and coordination among healthcare providers, administrative staff, and patients. Additionally, they leveraged cloud-based electronic health record (EHR) systems to ensure secure access to patient data from any location.

By embracing technology and adopting agile practices, the healthcare organization successfully adapted to the changing landscape, ensuring the delivery of essential healthcare services while safeguarding the well-being of patients and staff. This case study highlights the importance of agility, innovation, and resilience in responding to crisis situations and driving organizational resilience.

In summary, lessons learned and best practices from case studies offer valuable insights into the complexities of real-world challenges and the strategies employed to overcome them. By studying successful initiatives across various industries, organizations can glean actionable insights, identify common pitfalls, and adopt proven approaches to drive their own success. Through continuous learning, adaptation, and improvement, organizations can navigate uncertainty, seize opportunities, and thrive in an ever-changing business environment.

BOOK 4
BEYOND BASICS
EXPERT INSIGHTS INTO SERVICE DESK MANAGEMENT
IN THE DIGITAL AGE

ROB BOTWRIGHT

Chapter 1: The Evolution of Service Desk Management in the Digital Era

The historical overview of service desk evolution traces back to the early days of computing when mainframe computers dominated the landscape. During this era, service desks primarily functioned as help desks, providing basic technical support and troubleshooting assistance to users encountering issues with their hardware or software. These early help desks were typically staffed by a small team of IT professionals who fielded phone calls or responded to emails from users seeking assistance.

As technology advanced and computing became more prevalent in businesses and organizations, the role of the service desk evolved to encompass a broader range of responsibilities. With the advent of client-server architecture and the proliferation of personal computers in the workplace, service desks began to handle a more diverse set of tasks, including software installations, network connectivity issues, and user account management.

During the 1990s, the concept of IT service management (ITSM) emerged as a structured approach to delivering and managing IT services within organizations. This period saw the formalization of IT service processes and the adoption of frameworks such as IT Infrastructure Library (ITIL) to standardize service delivery practices. Service desks, now recognized as integral components of ITSM, played a central role in implementing ITIL best practices and ensuring the efficient operation of IT services.

The early 2000s witnessed significant advancements in technology, with the widespread adoption of the internet, mobile devices, and cloud computing transforming the IT landscape. These technological developments necessitated a shift in the role of the service desk from a reactive support function to a proactive enabler of business operations. Service desks began to focus on delivering value-added services, such as remote support, self-service portals, and knowledge management systems, to enhance user experience and improve service delivery efficiency.

The rise of ITIL as a de facto standard for IT service management further influenced the evolution of service desks, with organizations increasingly aligning their service desk operations with ITIL principles and frameworks. This alignment enabled service desks to adopt a structured approach to service delivery, incorporating processes such as incident management, problem management, change management, and service level management to ensure the reliable and consistent delivery of IT services.

In recent years, the advent of digital transformation and the proliferation of disruptive technologies such as artificial intelligence (AI), machine learning, and automation have further reshaped the service desk landscape. Organizations are leveraging these technologies to streamline service desk operations, enhance service quality, and improve the overall user experience. AI-powered chatbots, for example, are increasingly being deployed to handle routine service desk inquiries, freeing up human agents to focus on more complex issues.

Moreover, the COVID-19 pandemic accelerated the adoption of remote work practices, prompting organizations to rethink their service desk strategies to support distributed workforces effectively. Service desks quickly adapted to the new normal by deploying remote support tools, virtual collaboration platforms, and self-service portals to facilitate seamless communication and collaboration among remote teams and users.

Looking ahead, the evolution of service desks is expected to continue as organizations embrace emerging technologies and evolving service delivery models. Service desks will play a crucial role in driving digital transformation initiatives, leveraging data analytics, AI, and automation to deliver proactive, personalized, and efficient support services. By staying abreast of technological advancements and evolving customer expectations, service desks can remain agile and responsive in meeting the ever-changing demands of the digital age.

The impact of digital transformation on service desk management is profound and multifaceted, reshaping traditional practices and necessitating a paradigm shift in how organizations deliver IT support services. As businesses undergo digital transformation initiatives to remain competitive and meet evolving customer expectations, the role of the service desk is evolving from a reactive support function to a strategic enabler of digital innovation. This transformation is driven by advancements in technology, changes in business processes, and shifts in customer preferences, all of which are fundamentally altering the way service desks operate and deliver value to organizations.

One of the most significant impacts of digital transformation on service desk management is the increasing complexity and diversity of IT environments. With the proliferation of cloud computing, mobile devices, Internet of Things (IoT) devices, and software-as-a-service (SaaS) applications, organizations are managing a broader array of technologies and platforms than ever before. This complexity presents unique challenges for service desks, requiring them to support a diverse range of devices, applications, and environments while ensuring seamless integration and interoperability across the IT ecosystem.

To address these challenges, organizations are adopting integrated service management platforms that provide a unified view of IT infrastructure and services, allowing service desks to efficiently monitor, manage, and support complex IT environments. These platforms often include features such as incident management, problem management, change management, and configuration management, enabling service desks to streamline IT service delivery processes and improve operational efficiency.

Another key impact of digital transformation on service desk management is the growing demand for personalized and proactive support services. In today's digital age, users expect fast, convenient, and personalized support experiences tailored to their specific needs and preferences. To meet these expectations, service desks are leveraging technologies such as AI, machine learning, and natural language processing to deliver more intelligent and proactive support services.

For example, AI-powered chatbots and virtual assistants are being deployed to provide instant assistance and automate routine support tasks, such as password resets, software installations, and knowledge base searches. These intelligent assistants can analyze user queries, identify patterns, and provide relevant solutions in real-time, reducing response times and improving overall service desk efficiency.

Moreover, digital transformation is driving a shift towards self-service support models, empowering users to resolve issues independently without the need for human intervention. Self-service portals, knowledge bases, and online forums enable users to access information, troubleshoot common issues, and request assistance on their own terms, reducing reliance on the service desk for routine inquiries and freeing up agents to focus on more complex tasks.

In addition to enhancing support capabilities, digital transformation is also enabling service desks to adopt a more proactive and predictive approach to IT service management. By leveraging data analytics and predictive analytics, service desks can analyze historical trends, identify potential issues before they occur, and take proactive measures to prevent service disruptions and minimize downtime.

For instance, predictive analytics can help service desks anticipate hardware failures, software glitches, and network outages by analyzing patterns in system performance data and alerting IT teams to potential issues in real-time. This proactive approach not only improves service desk efficiency but also enhances the overall reliability and availability of IT services, leading to higher levels of customer satisfaction and business productivity.

Furthermore, digital transformation is driving a cultural shift within organizations, fostering collaboration, agility, and innovation across IT and business functions. Service desks are increasingly viewed as strategic partners that contribute to business growth and competitiveness by enabling digital innovation, driving process improvements, and delivering exceptional customer experiences.

To capitalize on the opportunities presented by digital transformation, organizations must invest in the right people, processes, and technologies to empower their service desks to thrive in the digital age. This includes providing ongoing training and professional development opportunities for service desk staff, implementing robust IT service management frameworks and best practices, and leveraging cutting-edge technologies to automate repetitive tasks, streamline workflows, and enhance the overall service desk experience.

In summary, the impact of digital transformation on service desk management is profound and far-reaching, reshaping traditional support practices and driving a shift towards more personalized, proactive, and efficient service delivery models. By embracing digital innovation, organizations can empower their service desks to become strategic enablers of business success, driving growth, innovation, and customer satisfaction in the digital age.

Chapter 2: Leveraging AI and Automation in Service Desk Operations

The role of Artificial Intelligence (AI) in service desk operations is increasingly prominent, revolutionizing traditional support processes and enhancing the efficiency and effectiveness of IT service delivery. AI technologies, including machine learning, natural language processing (NLP), and chatbots, are being leveraged to automate routine tasks, streamline workflows, and provide intelligent assistance to users, thereby transforming the way service desks operate and deliver value to organizations.

One of the primary applications of AI in service desk operations is the deployment of AI-powered chatbots to provide instant support and assistance to users. Chatbots utilize NLP algorithms to understand user queries and provide relevant responses or solutions in real-time. By integrating chatbots into service desk workflows, organizations can improve response times, reduce support costs, and enhance the overall user experience.

To deploy an AI-powered chatbot in service desk operations, organizations can utilize platforms such as Microsoft Azure Bot Service, Google Dialogflow, or IBM Watson Assistant. These platforms provide tools and frameworks for building, training, and deploying chatbots that can understand natural language queries, integrate with backend systems and databases, and provide intelligent responses to users. For example, organizations can use the Microsoft Azure Bot Service to create a chatbot that integrates with Microsoft Teams or Slack to provide instant support to users within their preferred communication channels.

Another key role of AI in service desk operations is the automation of routine support tasks, such as password resets, software installations, and knowledge base searches. By leveraging machine learning algorithms, organizations can automate these tasks, freeing up service desk agents to focus on more complex and value-added activities. For example, AI-powered automation tools can analyze incoming support tickets, identify repetitive tasks, and automatically execute predefined workflows or scripts to resolve common issues without human intervention.

To implement AI-powered automation in service desk operations, organizations can utilize tools such as Puppet, Ansible, or Chef for configuration management and orchestration. These tools allow organizations to define and automate IT infrastructure tasks, such as provisioning servers, deploying applications, and configuring network settings, using declarative configuration files or scripts. For example, organizations can use Ansible playbooks to automate software installations and configuration changes across their IT infrastructure, reducing manual effort and ensuring consistency and reliability.

Furthermore, AI technologies are being used to augment the capabilities of service desk agents, providing them with real-time insights, recommendations, and predictive analytics to improve decision-making and problem-solving. For example, AI-powered analytics tools can analyze historical support data, identify patterns and trends, and provide service desk agents with recommendations for resolving issues more effectively. Similarly, AI-driven knowledge management systems can suggest relevant articles, documents, or solutions based on the context of the user query, enabling service desk agents to quickly access the information they need to assist users.

To implement AI-driven analytics and knowledge management in service desk operations, organizations can leverage platforms such as Splunk, Elasticsearch, or IBM Watson Discovery. These platforms provide capabilities for ingesting, analyzing, and visualizing large volumes of data from diverse sources, enabling organizations to derive actionable insights and make informed decisions. For example, organizations can use Splunk to analyze service desk logs and identify trends or anomalies that may indicate underlying issues or opportunities for improvement.

In addition to improving operational efficiency and customer satisfaction, AI technologies are also helping service desks to enhance security and compliance by identifying and mitigating potential risks and vulnerabilities in real-time. For example, AI-driven security tools can analyze network traffic, detect suspicious activities or anomalies, and alert service desk teams to potential security incidents or breaches. Similarly, AI-powered compliance management systems can automate the process of monitoring and enforcing regulatory requirements, ensuring that organizations remain compliant with industry standards and regulations.

To implement AI-driven security and compliance management in service desk operations, organizations can utilize tools such as Splunk Enterprise Security, IBM QRadar, or Palo Alto Networks Cortex XDR. These platforms provide capabilities for threat detection, incident response, and compliance reporting, enabling organizations to proactively identify and address security risks and ensure regulatory compliance. For example, organizations can use Splunk Enterprise Security to analyze security logs and detect anomalous behavior that may indicate a potential security threat, allowing them to take timely action to mitigate the risk.

In summary, the role of Artificial Intelligence (AI) in service desk operations is becoming increasingly important, enabling organizations to automate routine tasks, enhance decision-making, and improve overall service delivery. By leveraging AI technologies such as chatbots, automation, analytics, and security, organizations can streamline support processes, reduce costs, and deliver a more intelligent and personalized experience to users, thereby driving greater efficiency, productivity, and customer satisfaction.

Implementing automation for efficiency and scalability is essential for modern organizations seeking to streamline workflows, improve productivity, and adapt to changing business demands. Automation encompasses a wide range of technologies and techniques that enable organizations to automate repetitive tasks, standardize processes, and orchestrate complex workflows across their IT infrastructure and business operations. By leveraging automation, organizations can reduce manual effort, minimize errors, and accelerate time-to-market, ultimately driving greater efficiency and scalability across the organization.

One of the fundamental principles of automation is the use of scripting and configuration management tools to automate routine tasks and standardize configurations across heterogeneous environments. Command Line Interface (CLI) commands are often used to execute scripts and perform configuration tasks programmatically, enabling organizations to automate repetitive tasks such as software provisioning, configuration changes, and system monitoring. For example, organizations can use the **bash** shell scripting language on Linux-based systems to write scripts that automate routine administrative tasks, such as user management, file system operations, and system backups.

To deploy automation scripts in production environments, organizations typically use version control systems such as Git to manage and track changes to their scripts and configuration files. By using Git, organizations can collaborate with multiple team members, track changes over time, and roll back to previous versions if needed. For example, organizations can use the **git clone**, **git add**, **git commit**, and **git push** commands to clone a repository, stage changes, commit them to the repository, and push them to a remote server, respectively.

In addition to scripting and configuration management, organizations can also leverage automation tools and platforms to orchestrate complex workflows and streamline cross-functional processes. Workflow automation platforms such as Ansible, Puppet, and Chef enable organizations to define and automate multi-step workflows, from provisioning infrastructure resources to deploying applications and configuring software components. These platforms provide libraries of pre-built modules and playbooks that can be customized and reused to automate common tasks and processes. For example, organizations can use Ansible playbooks to automate the deployment of web applications across multiple servers, ensuring consistency and reliability.

To deploy automation workflows using Ansible, organizations typically install the Ansible software on a control node and configure it to communicate with managed nodes using SSH or WinRM (Windows Remote Management). Once Ansible is installed, organizations can define automation tasks and workflows using YAML-based playbooks, which specify the desired state of the system and the tasks required to achieve that state. For example, organizations can use the **ansible-playbook** command to execute an Ansible playbook and automate tasks such as package installation, service configuration, and file management across their infrastructure.

Furthermore, organizations can leverage Infrastructure as Code (IaC) principles and tools to automate the provisioning and management of infrastructure resources using code-based templates and configurations. IaC tools such as Terraform, AWS CloudFormation, and Azure Resource Manager enable organizations to define infrastructure resources declaratively using code, which can then be versioned, tested, and deployed programmatically. These tools provide a high level of abstraction and automation, allowing organizations to provision and manage infrastructure resources such as virtual machines, networks, and storage using code-based templates. For example, organizations can use Terraform configuration files to define and provision infrastructure resources on public cloud platforms such as AWS, Azure, and Google Cloud Platform (GCP).

To deploy infrastructure resources using Terraform, organizations typically define their infrastructure configurations in Terraform configuration files (usually with a **.tf** extension) and use the **terraform init**, **terraform plan**, and **terraform apply** commands to initialize the Terraform environment, generate an execution plan, and apply the changes to the infrastructure, respectively. For example, organizations can use the **terraform init** command to initialize the Terraform environment in a project directory and the **terraform apply** command to apply the changes defined in the Terraform configuration files to the infrastructure.

Moreover, organizations can leverage containerization and orchestration platforms such as Docker and Kubernetes to automate the deployment, scaling, and management of containerized applications across distributed environments. Containerization enables organizations to package applications and their dependencies into lightweight, portable containers, which can then be deployed and run consistently across different environments. Kubernetes, an open-source container orchestration platform, provides automated deployment, scaling, and management of containerized applications, allowing organizations to automate the deployment and scaling of applications based on resource utilization and demand. For example, organizations can use Docker to containerize their applications and Kubernetes to deploy and manage them in production environments.

To deploy containerized applications using Kubernetes, organizations typically define their application configurations in Kubernetes manifests (usually with a **.yaml** extension) and use the **kubectl** command-line tool to interact with the Kubernetes cluster. For example, organizations can use the **kubectl apply** command to apply the Kubernetes manifests to the cluster and deploy the specified resources, such as pods, services, and deployments. Additionally, organizations can use the **kubectl scale** command to scale the number of replicas for a deployment based on demand, ensuring optimal resource utilization and performance.

Chapter 3: Implementing Self-Service and Chatbots for Enhanced User Experience

Self-service solutions in service desk management offer a plethora of benefits that significantly enhance operational efficiency, user satisfaction, and overall organizational productivity. These solutions empower users to address their own IT issues and requests independently, reducing the burden on service desk staff and enabling them to focus on more complex tasks and strategic initiatives. One of the primary advantages of self-service solutions is the ability to provide round-the-clock support to users, irrespective of their location or time zone. Users can access self-service portals or knowledge bases at any time to find solutions to their IT issues or submit requests for assistance, eliminating the need to wait for traditional service desk support hours to receive assistance.

Moreover, self-service solutions facilitate faster resolution of IT issues and requests by providing users with instant access to relevant information and resources. Instead of waiting in a queue for assistance from a service desk agent, users can quickly search for solutions to their problems in the self-service knowledge base or follow guided troubleshooting steps to resolve common issues independently. For example, if a user encounters a software installation problem, they can access the self-service portal, search for relevant articles or guides on software installation troubleshooting, and follow the step-by-step instructions to resolve the issue without needing to contact the service desk.

Another key benefit of self-service solutions is their ability to promote user empowerment and autonomy. By providing users with the tools and resources they need to address their own IT needs, organizations empower users to take ownership of their IT experience and become more self-sufficient in managing their technology-related issues and requests. This not only reduces dependency on the service desk but also fosters a culture of self-reliance and continuous learning among users. Additionally, self-service solutions can help improve user satisfaction by providing a more convenient and personalized support experience. Users appreciate the flexibility and convenience of being able to resolve their own IT issues or submit requests for assistance at their own pace and on their own schedule, without having to wait for assistance from a service desk agent.

Furthermore, self-service solutions contribute to cost savings and operational efficiency by reducing the volume of incoming support tickets and inquiries handled by the service desk. By automating routine tasks and providing users with self-help resources, organizations can streamline their support processes, optimize resource allocation, and minimize the need for manual intervention from service desk staff. This allows organizations to reallocate their service desk resources to more strategic initiatives and high-value activities that drive business growth and innovation. Additionally, self-service solutions enable organizations to scale their support operations more effectively to meet growing demand without significantly increasing staffing levels or operational costs.

Another significant advantage of self-service solutions is their ability to capture and leverage valuable data and insights about user behavior, preferences, and common IT issues. By analyzing self-service usage data, organizations can identify trends, patterns, and recurring issues that may require further attention or intervention. This insight can inform proactive service improvement initiatives, such as updating knowledge base articles, creating new self-help resources, or implementing automated workflows to address common issues more effectively. Additionally, self-service solutions can integrate with other ITSM tools and systems to provide a seamless support experience and facilitate end-to-end service delivery and management.

In summary, self-service solutions play a crucial role in modern service desk management by empowering users, enhancing operational efficiency, and driving organizational productivity. By providing users with instant access to relevant information and resources, promoting user empowerment and autonomy, reducing support costs, and capturing valuable insights, self-service solutions enable organizations to deliver a superior support experience and achieve their business objectives more effectively. As organizations continue to embrace digital transformation and prioritize user-centric support models, self-service solutions will remain a cornerstone of effective service desk management strategies.

Designing effective chatbot solutions for user support is crucial in today's digital age, where organizations strive to provide seamless and efficient customer service experiences. Chatbots, powered by artificial intelligence (AI) and natural language processing (NLP) technologies, have emerged as valuable tools for automating repetitive tasks, providing instant responses to user inquiries, and delivering personalized support around the clock. However, creating successful chatbot solutions requires careful planning, thoughtful design, and ongoing optimization to ensure they meet user needs and deliver tangible business value.

The first step in designing effective chatbot solutions is to define clear objectives and use cases based on the specific needs and challenges of the organization. This involves identifying the types of inquiries and tasks that the chatbot will handle, such as answering frequently asked questions, providing product information, troubleshooting technical issues, or assisting with account management. By understanding the scope and purpose of the chatbot, organizations can tailor its functionality and capabilities to align with user expectations and business objectives.

Once the objectives and use cases are defined, organizations can begin designing the conversation flow and user experience (UX) of the chatbot. This involves mapping out various user interactions and designing conversational scripts that guide users through different scenarios and tasks. It's essential to ensure that the chatbot's responses are clear, concise, and contextually relevant to provide users with accurate information and assistance. Additionally, organizations should consider incorporating personality traits and brand voice into the chatbot's communication style to create a more engaging and memorable experience for users.

In terms of deployment, organizations can leverage a variety of platforms and tools to build and deploy chatbot solutions. One popular option is to use chatbot development frameworks and platforms that provide pre-built templates, integrations, and NLP capabilities to streamline the development process. For example, developers can use frameworks like Microsoft Bot Framework, Google Dialogflow, or IBM Watson Assistant to build chatbots that can understand and respond to user queries in natural language.

Once the chatbot is built, organizations need to train and test it thoroughly to ensure it performs effectively in real-world scenarios. This involves training the chatbot's AI models with relevant data sets and examples to improve its accuracy and understanding of user intents. Additionally, organizations should conduct user testing and feedback sessions to gather insights into the chatbot's performance and identify areas for improvement. By iterating on the design and functionality based on user feedback, organizations can refine the chatbot's capabilities and enhance its overall effectiveness.

Furthermore, organizations should consider integrating the chatbot with other systems and channels to provide a seamless omnichannel support experience. For example, the chatbot can be integrated with CRM systems, ticketing platforms, knowledge bases, and social media channels to access relevant user data, provide personalized recommendations, and escalate inquiries to human agents when necessary. Integrating the chatbot with these systems allows organizations to leverage existing resources and infrastructure to deliver more comprehensive and efficient support solutions.

In terms of monitoring and optimization, organizations should implement analytics and reporting mechanisms to track key performance metrics and gather insights into the chatbot's usage, effectiveness, and user satisfaction. This involves monitoring metrics such as response times, conversation completion rates, user engagement, and customer feedback to identify areas for improvement and optimization. By analyzing these metrics regularly, organizations can identify trends, patterns, and opportunities to enhance the chatbot's performance and deliver a better user experience.

In summary, designing effective chatbot solutions for user support requires careful planning, thoughtful design, and ongoing optimization to ensure they meet user needs and deliver tangible business value. By defining clear objectives and use cases, designing intuitive conversation flows and UX, leveraging appropriate development platforms and tools, training and testing the chatbot thoroughly, integrating with other systems and channels, and monitoring and optimizing performance continuously, organizations can create chatbot solutions that provide valuable support to users and drive business success.

Chapter 4: Integrating Service Desk with DevOps and Agile Methodologies

Alignment of service desk practices with DevOps principles is essential for organizations seeking to streamline their IT operations, enhance collaboration between development and operations teams, and accelerate the delivery of high-quality software products and services. DevOps, a cultural and organizational movement aimed at breaking down silos, fostering collaboration, and promoting automation throughout the software development lifecycle, emphasizes principles such as continuous integration, continuous delivery, infrastructure as code, and automated testing. By aligning service desk practices with these principles, organizations can improve incident response times, increase operational efficiency, and deliver better outcomes for both internal and external customers.

One of the key principles of DevOps is continuous integration (CI), which involves automatically integrating code changes into a shared repository multiple times a day. This practice helps teams identify and address integration issues early in the development process, reducing the risk of conflicts and ensuring that changes are thoroughly tested before deployment. Service desks can align with CI practices by implementing automated incident management workflows that integrate seamlessly with CI/CD pipelines. For example, organizations can use tools like Jenkins, GitLab CI/CD, or CircleCI to trigger incident alerts and automatically assign tasks to the appropriate teams whenever a build or deployment fails. By automating incident detection and response, service desks can minimize downtime and accelerate the resolution of issues.

Another DevOps principle that service desks can align with is continuous delivery (CD), which involves automating the deployment of code changes to production environments. CD practices enable organizations to release software updates quickly, reliably, and frequently, reducing the time to market and increasing agility. Service desks can support CD initiatives by implementing self-service incident resolution processes and leveraging automation tools to streamline change management workflows. For example, organizations can use infrastructure as code (IaC) tools like Terraform or Ansible to automate the provisioning and configuration of infrastructure resources, allowing development teams to deploy changes consistently and predictably across different environments. By adopting CD practices, service desks can facilitate faster and more reliable deployments, enabling teams to deliver value to customers more frequently.

In addition to CI/CD practices, service desks can also align with DevOps principles by embracing a culture of collaboration, transparency, and shared responsibility. DevOps emphasizes the importance of breaking down organizational silos and promoting cross-functional teamwork, with the goal of fostering a culture of continuous improvement and innovation. Service desks can support this culture by implementing collaborative incident management processes that encourage communication and knowledge sharing across teams. For example, organizations can use incident management platforms like PagerDuty, ServiceNow, or Jira Service Management to centralize incident information, facilitate real-time communication between stakeholders, and capture post-incident learnings for future reference. By promoting collaboration and shared responsibility, service desks can help build trust and alignment between development and operations teams, leading to better outcomes for the organization as a whole.

Furthermore, service desks can align with DevOps principles by adopting practices such as infrastructure as code (IaC), automated testing, and monitoring as code. IaC involves managing infrastructure resources programmatically using declarative configuration files, allowing organizations to treat infrastructure as software and apply software development best practices such as version control, code review, and automated testing. Service desks can support IaC initiatives by providing guidance and support for teams adopting infrastructure automation tools and practices. For example, organizations can use tools like AWS CloudFormation, Terraform, or Azure Resource Manager to define and provision infrastructure resources using code, enabling teams to manage infrastructure changes more effectively and consistently. By promoting IaC practices, service desks can help organizations improve agility, reduce manual overhead, and increase infrastructure reliability.

Automated testing is another DevOps practice that service desks can align with to improve the quality and reliability of software deployments. Automated testing involves running tests automatically against code changes to validate functionality, performance, and security before deployment. Service desks can support automated testing initiatives by providing access to testing environments, tools, and resources, as well as facilitating collaboration between development and testing teams. For example, organizations can use test automation frameworks like Selenium, JUnit, or pytest to automate the execution of unit tests, integration tests, and end-to-end tests, allowing teams to identify and fix issues early in the development process. By promoting automated testing practices, service desks can help organizations reduce the risk of defects and vulnerabilities in production environments, leading to higher customer satisfaction and retention.

Monitoring as code is another DevOps practice that service desks can align with to improve visibility, observability, and troubleshooting capabilities in production environments. Monitoring as code involves defining and managing monitoring configurations using code, allowing organizations to treat monitoring infrastructure as software and apply software development best practices such as version control, code review, and automated deployment. Service desks can support monitoring as code initiatives by providing guidance and support for teams adopting monitoring automation tools and practices. For example, organizations can use tools like Prometheus, Grafana, or Datadog to define monitoring alerts, dashboards, and metrics using code, enabling teams to deploy and manage monitoring configurations more efficiently and consistently. By promoting monitoring as code practices, service desks can help organizations improve incident detection and response times, leading to faster issue resolution and reduced impact on customers.

adopting CI/CD practices, embracing a culture of collaboration and shared responsibility, and leveraging automation tools and techniques, service desks can enhance incident response times, increase operational efficiency, and deliver better outcomes for both internal and external customers. Agile approach to service desk management and delivery is another critical aspect that organizations can adopt to further improve their IT service delivery capabilities.

Agile methodology, originally developed for software development, emphasizes iterative development, continuous feedback, and rapid response to change. By applying Agile principles to service desk management and delivery, organizations can adapt more quickly to evolving customer needs, improve team collaboration, and increase overall productivity. One of the key principles of Agile is prioritizing customer satisfaction through early and continuous delivery of valuable solutions. Service desks can align with this principle by implementing Agile practices such as backlog refinement, sprint planning, and iterative delivery of service improvements.

Backlog refinement is an Agile practice that involves regularly reviewing and prioritizing the list of work items, or backlog, to ensure that the most valuable and important tasks are addressed first. Service desks can use backlog refinement sessions to review incoming incidents, service requests, and other work items, prioritize them based on their impact and urgency, and ensure that the team is focused on delivering the highest value solutions to customers. For example, teams can use tools like Jira or Trello to maintain a backlog of service desk tickets, categorize them based on their severity and impact, and regularly review and update the backlog to reflect changing priorities.

Sprint planning is another Agile practice that service desks can adopt to improve their delivery process. Sprint planning involves setting goals and defining the scope of work for a fixed period, or sprint, typically two to four weeks long. During sprint planning sessions, the service desk team collaborates to select a set of work items from the backlog that they commit to completing during the sprint. By breaking down work items into smaller, more manageable tasks and estimating their effort, teams can better plan and allocate resources, track progress, and deliver value to customers more consistently. For example, teams can use tools like Scrum or Kanban boards to visualize their workflow, track the status of work items, and identify bottlenecks or areas for improvement.

Iterative delivery is a core principle of Agile methodology that emphasizes delivering working solutions to customers frequently and incrementally. Service desks can apply this principle by adopting a "fail fast, learn fast" mindset and continuously iterating on their service offerings based on customer feedback and changing requirements. For example, instead of waiting to implement large, complex changes, teams can break down work items into smaller, more manageable tasks and deliver them to customers as soon as they are ready. By soliciting feedback early and often, teams can identify areas for improvement and make course corrections quickly, leading to better outcomes for customers and higher levels of satisfaction.

In addition to backlog refinement, sprint planning, and iterative delivery, service desks can also benefit from other Agile practices such as daily stand-up meetings, retrospectives, and continuous improvement. Daily stand-up meetings, or "daily scrums," provide an opportunity for team members to synchronize their activities, discuss progress, and identify any obstacles or impediments that need to be addressed. Retrospectives, held at the end of each sprint, allow teams to reflect on their performance, identify successes and areas for improvement, and make actionable plans for the next sprint. Continuous improvement involves regularly reviewing and refining processes, tools, and practices to ensure that the team is always striving to deliver better outcomes for customers.

By adopting an Agile approach to service desk management and delivery, organizations can improve their ability to respond quickly to changing customer needs, increase collaboration and transparency within the team, and deliver value to customers more consistently. By incorporating Agile practices such as backlog refinement, sprint planning, iterative delivery, daily stand-up meetings, retrospectives, and continuous improvement, service desks can enhance their agility, resilience, and overall effectiveness in delivering IT services.

Chapter 5: Cybersecurity Considerations for Modern Service Desk Managers

Understanding cybersecurity risks in service desk operations is paramount in today's digital landscape, where organizations face a multitude of threats that can compromise sensitive information, disrupt operations, and damage reputation. Service desks, as the frontline of IT support, are often targeted by cybercriminals seeking to exploit vulnerabilities and gain unauthorized access to systems and data. By comprehensively understanding these risks and implementing appropriate measures to mitigate them, organizations can safeguard their assets, maintain trust with customers, and ensure business continuity.

One of the primary cybersecurity risks in service desk operations is social engineering attacks, where attackers manipulate individuals into divulging sensitive information or performing actions that compromise security. Common examples include phishing, where attackers impersonate legitimate entities to trick users into revealing login credentials or clicking on malicious links, and pretexting, where attackers fabricate scenarios to elicit sensitive information from unsuspecting individuals. To mitigate these risks, organizations should conduct regular security awareness training for service desk staff, teaching them how to recognize and respond to social engineering attacks, and implement email filtering and spam detection solutions to block malicious emails before they reach users' inboxes.

Another significant cybersecurity risk in service desk operations is credential theft, where attackers steal user credentials to gain unauthorized access to systems and data. This can occur through various means, such as brute-force attacks, where attackers repeatedly guess passwords until they find the correct one, or credential stuffing attacks, where attackers use stolen credentials from one site to attempt to log in to other sites. To mitigate these risks, organizations should enforce strong password policies, requiring users to use complex passwords and enabling multi-factor authentication (MFA) to add an extra layer of security. Additionally, organizations should regularly monitor and analyze authentication logs for signs of suspicious activity, such as multiple failed login attempts or logins from unusual locations.

Malware and ransomware pose another significant cybersecurity risk to service desk operations, with attackers using malicious software to compromise systems, steal data, or extort money from victims. Malware can be delivered through various vectors, including email attachments, malicious websites, and removable media, and can cause significant damage if not detected and mitigated promptly. To mitigate these risks, organizations should deploy antivirus and antimalware solutions on all endpoints, regularly update software and operating systems to patch known vulnerabilities, and implement network security measures such as firewalls and intrusion detection systems (IDS) to detect and block malicious traffic.

Data breaches are also a significant cybersecurity risk in service desk operations, where attackers gain unauthorized access to sensitive information, such as customer data, intellectual property, or financial records. Data breaches can have severe consequences for organizations, including financial losses, legal liabilities, and reputational damage. To mitigate these risks, organizations should implement robust data protection measures, such as encryption, access controls, and data loss prevention (DLP) solutions, to ensure that sensitive information is adequately protected from unauthorized access or disclosure. Additionally, organizations should establish incident response plans and procedures to detect, contain, and respond to data breaches effectively, minimizing their impact on the business and affected individuals.

Insider threats also pose a significant cybersecurity risk to service desk operations, where trusted insiders, such as employees, contractors, or business partners, intentionally or unintentionally compromise security. Insider threats can take various forms, including malicious insiders who deliberately steal or leak sensitive information and negligent insiders who inadvertently expose data through careless actions or negligence. To mitigate these risks, organizations should implement strong access controls and user monitoring mechanisms to restrict access to sensitive information and detect anomalous behavior. Additionally, organizations should provide regular cybersecurity training and awareness programs for employees, educating them about the importance of security best practices and the consequences of insider threats.

Supply chain attacks represent another significant cybersecurity risk in service desk operations, where attackers compromise third-party vendors or suppliers to gain unauthorized access to an organization's systems and data. These attacks can occur through various means, such as compromising software supply chains, exploiting vulnerabilities in third-party services, or targeting trusted partners with phishing or social engineering attacks. To mitigate these risks, organizations should conduct thorough due diligence when selecting and vetting third-party vendors or suppliers, ensuring that they have robust security practices and controls in place. Additionally, organizations should implement monitoring and auditing mechanisms to detect and respond to suspicious activity or unauthorized access by third parties.

In summary, understanding cybersecurity risks in service desk operations is essential for organizations to effectively mitigate threats, protect sensitive information, and ensure business continuity. By implementing robust security measures, such as security awareness training, strong authentication mechanisms, endpoint protection, data encryption, access controls, and incident response plans, organizations can reduce their risk exposure and safeguard their assets against cyber threats. Additionally, organizations should stay informed about emerging threats and best practices in cybersecurity to adapt their security posture accordingly and stay ahead of evolving threats in an increasingly digital world.

Implementing security best practices in service desk management is crucial for organizations to protect sensitive information, maintain the confidentiality, integrity, and availability of data, and mitigate cybersecurity risks effectively. Service desks, as the central point of contact for IT support, play a critical role in ensuring that security policies and procedures are enforced consistently across the organization. By implementing a robust framework of security best practices, organizations can enhance their security posture, minimize the likelihood of security incidents, and safeguard their assets from potential threats.

One of the fundamental security best practices in service desk management is enforcing strong authentication mechanisms to verify the identity of users and control access to sensitive information and systems. This includes implementing multi-factor authentication (MFA), which requires users to provide two or more forms of authentication before granting access to resources. CLI commands like **passwd** in Linux or **Set-ADAccountPassword** in Windows Server can be used to enforce password policies and enable MFA for user accounts, ensuring that unauthorized users cannot gain access even if their passwords are compromised.

Another essential security best practice is regularly updating and patching software and systems to address known vulnerabilities and protect against security exploits. This includes applying security patches and updates promptly, conducting regular vulnerability assessments and scans, and implementing a patch management process to prioritize and deploy patches efficiently. CLI commands like **apt update** and **apt upgrade** in Linux or **Update-Help** and **Install-Module** in PowerShell can be used to update software packages and install security patches, ensuring that systems are protected against known vulnerabilities.

Organizations should also implement robust access controls and authorization mechanisms to limit access to sensitive information and systems based on the principle of least privilege. This involves granting users only the permissions necessary to perform their job functions and restricting access to critical resources to authorized personnel only. CLI commands like **chmod** and **chown** in Linux or **Get-Acl** and **Set-Acl** in PowerShell can be used to configure file and directory permissions, ensuring that only authorized users can access sensitive data.

Encryption is another critical security best practice that organizations should implement to protect data both at rest and in transit. This involves encrypting sensitive data using cryptographic algorithms to prevent unauthorized access or disclosure. CLI commands like **openssl** in Linux or **Encrypt-File** and **Protect-CmsMessage** in PowerShell can be used to encrypt files and communications, ensuring that sensitive information remains secure even if it is intercepted or accessed by unauthorized parties.

Implementing robust incident response and security incident management processes is essential for effectively detecting, responding to, and mitigating security incidents and breaches. This includes establishing incident response teams, defining escalation procedures, and conducting regular incident response drills and exercises to test the effectiveness of security controls and procedures. CLI commands like **grep** and **awk** in Linux or **Get-WinEvent** and **New-EventLog** in PowerShell can be used to search for and analyze security logs, identify indicators of compromise, and investigate security incidents effectively.

Regular security awareness training and education programs are also essential for ensuring that service desk staff are aware of security risks and best practices and are equipped to identify and respond to security threats effectively. This includes providing training on topics such as phishing awareness, password security, data protection, and incident response procedures. CLI commands like **curl** and **wget** in Linux or **Invoke-WebRequest** and **Send-MailMessage** in PowerShell can be used to simulate phishing attacks and deliver security awareness training to service desk staff, helping them recognize and respond to security threats effectively.

Organizations should also implement robust physical security measures to protect service desk facilities and equipment from unauthorized access, theft, or tampering. This includes restricting access to service desk areas, implementing surveillance cameras and access control systems, and securing hardware devices and peripherals to prevent unauthorized use or removal. CLI commands like **sudo** and **iptables** in Linux or **Get-PhysicalDisk** and **Set-PhysicalDisk** in PowerShell can be used to configure access controls and security policies, ensuring that only authorized personnel can access service desk facilities and equipment.

In summary, implementing security best practices in service desk management is essential for organizations to protect sensitive information, mitigate cybersecurity risks, and maintain the confidentiality, integrity, and availability of data. By enforcing strong authentication mechanisms, regularly updating and patching software, implementing access controls and encryption, establishing incident response processes, providing security awareness training, and implementing physical security measures, organizations can enhance their security posture and ensure that service desk operations are conducted in a secure and compliant manner.

Chapter 6: Managing Remote and Distributed Service Desk Teams

Managing remote service desk teams presents both challenges and opportunities for organizations in today's digital landscape. With the increasing trend towards remote work, service desk teams are often dispersed across different locations, requiring organizations to adopt new strategies and technologies to ensure efficient operations and effective customer support. One of the primary challenges faced by remote service desk teams is communication and collaboration. Unlike traditional office environments where team members can easily communicate face-to-face, remote teams rely heavily on digital communication tools and platforms to stay connected. This can lead to communication gaps, misunderstandings, and reduced team cohesion. However, organizations can overcome these challenges by implementing collaboration tools such as Slack, Microsoft Teams, or Zoom to facilitate real-time communication and collaboration among remote team members. These tools allow team members to chat, share files, and hold virtual meetings, helping to bridge the gap between remote workers and foster a sense of community and camaraderie.

Another challenge of managing remote service desk teams is maintaining productivity and accountability. Without direct supervision, remote team members may struggle to stay focused and motivated, leading to decreased productivity and performance. To address this challenge, organizations can implement productivity tracking tools such as Trello, Asana, or Jira to monitor team progress, track tasks, and identify potential bottlenecks. Additionally, setting clear expectations and goals for remote team members, providing regular feedback and recognition, and establishing regular check-ins and performance reviews can help keep remote workers accountable and motivated.

Ensuring data security and compliance is another significant challenge faced by remote service desk teams. With team members accessing sensitive information and systems from remote locations, organizations must implement robust security measures to protect data and mitigate cybersecurity risks. This includes implementing strong authentication mechanisms, encrypting sensitive data, and enforcing access controls and security policies. Organizations should also provide comprehensive security awareness training to remote team members to educate them about potential security threats and best practices for safeguarding data. Additionally, organizations must ensure compliance with relevant regulations and standards, such as GDPR or HIPAA, by implementing appropriate security controls and conducting regular audits and assessments.

Despite these challenges, remote service desk teams also present numerous opportunities for organizations to improve efficiency, flexibility, and scalability. By leveraging remote work technologies and practices, organizations can access a broader talent pool and attract top talent from around the world. Remote work allows organizations to hire skilled professionals regardless of their geographic location, enabling them to build diverse and inclusive teams with a wide range of expertise and experience. Additionally, remote work offers flexibility and autonomy to team members, allowing them to work at their own pace and schedule, which can lead to increased job satisfaction and work-life balance.

Remote service desk teams also offer opportunities for cost savings and resource optimization. By eliminating the need for physical office space and infrastructure, organizations can reduce overhead costs associated with office rent, utilities, and maintenance. Additionally, remote work allows organizations to optimize their workforce by scaling up or down as needed, depending on business demands. Organizations can hire contractors or freelancers for short-term projects or peak periods, without the need for long-term commitments or overhead expenses.

Furthermore, remote service desk teams enable organizations to improve customer service and support by providing round-the-clock coverage and faster response times. With team members spread across different time zones, organizations can ensure continuous support and minimize downtime for customers. Additionally, remote service desk teams can leverage technology such as AI-powered chatbots and self-service portals to automate routine tasks and provide instant assistance to customers, enhancing the overall customer experience.

In summary, while managing remote service desk teams presents its challenges, it also offers numerous opportunities for organizations to improve efficiency, flexibility, and scalability. By leveraging collaboration tools, ensuring productivity and accountability, maintaining data security and compliance, and embracing the benefits of remote work, organizations can overcome challenges and capitalize on the opportunities presented by remote service desk teams. With the right strategies and technologies in place, remote service desk teams can become a valuable asset for organizations, enabling them to deliver exceptional customer service and support in today's digital age.

Effective management of distributed teams is essential in today's globalized and digitalized work environment, where remote work has become increasingly prevalent. Distributed teams, comprised of members located in different geographic locations, present unique challenges related to communication, collaboration, and team cohesion. However, with the right strategies and tools in place, organizations can successfully manage distributed teams and maximize their productivity and performance.

One of the key strategies for effective management of distributed teams is establishing clear communication channels and protocols. Communication is the foundation of successful remote teamwork, and organizations must ensure that team members have access to reliable communication tools and platforms. Tools such as Slack, Microsoft Teams, or Zoom facilitate real-time communication through text, voice, and video, allowing team members to stay connected regardless of their location. Additionally, organizations should establish communication protocols, such as regular team meetings, daily stand-ups, and project updates, to ensure that important information is shared and team members are kept informed about project progress and changes.

Another important aspect of managing distributed teams is fostering a sense of collaboration and teamwork. Despite physical distance, team members should feel connected and engaged with each other, working towards common goals and objectives. Virtual team-building activities, such as virtual happy hours, online games, or collaborative projects, can help build rapport and strengthen relationships among team members. Additionally, organizations should encourage open communication and feedback, creating a culture of transparency and trust within the team. By fostering a collaborative environment, organizations can enhance team cohesion and productivity, despite the physical distance between team members.

Effective project management is also critical for managing distributed teams successfully. With team members located in different time zones and working asynchronously, organizations must adopt agile project management methodologies and tools to ensure that projects stay on track and deadlines are met. Tools such as Jira, Asana, or Trello allow teams to manage tasks, track progress, and prioritize work in a transparent and organized manner. Additionally, regular project reviews and retrospectives help identify bottlenecks and process improvements, allowing teams to continuously optimize their workflow and performance.

Managing performance and accountability is another challenge when it comes to distributed teams. Without direct supervision, team members may struggle to stay focused and motivated, leading to decreased productivity and performance. To address this challenge, organizations should set clear performance expectations and goals for remote team members, providing regular feedback and recognition for their achievements. Performance tracking tools, such as time tracking software or productivity dashboards, can help monitor individual and team performance, identify areas for improvement, and recognize top performers.

Ensuring data security and compliance is also a priority for managing distributed teams. With team members accessing sensitive information and systems from remote locations, organizations must implement robust security measures to protect data and mitigate cybersecurity risks. This includes implementing strong authentication mechanisms, encrypting sensitive data, and enforcing access controls and security policies. Organizations should also provide comprehensive security awareness training to remote team members to educate them about potential security threats and best practices for safeguarding data. Additionally, regular audits and assessments help ensure compliance with relevant regulations and standards, such as GDPR or HIPAA.

In summary, effective management of distributed teams requires a combination of clear communication, collaboration, project management, performance tracking, and security measures. By implementing these strategies and leveraging the right tools and technologies, organizations can overcome the challenges associated with managing distributed teams and unlock the full potential of remote work. With the right approach, distributed teams can be highly productive, innovative, and successful in today's digital work environment.

Chapter 7: Big Data Analytics for Service Desk Optimization

Utilizing big data for service desk performance analysis is becoming increasingly important in modern organizations seeking to enhance their IT service management practices. Big data refers to large volumes of structured and unstructured data that can be analyzed to extract valuable insights and patterns. In the context of service desk management, big data analytics can offer organizations valuable insights into the performance of their service desk operations, enabling them to identify trends, detect anomalies, and optimize their processes for improved efficiency and customer satisfaction.

One of the key benefits of utilizing big data for service desk performance analysis is the ability to gain deeper insights into customer behavior and service usage patterns. By analyzing large volumes of service desk data, including ticket logs, user interactions, and service requests, organizations can identify common issues, recurring problems, and peak usage periods. This information can help organizations better understand customer needs and preferences, enabling them to tailor their services and support processes accordingly.

To deploy big data analytics for service desk performance analysis, organizations can leverage a variety of tools and technologies. One popular tool for big data analytics is Apache Hadoop, an open-source framework that allows organizations to store, process, and analyze large datasets across distributed computing clusters. Organizations can use Hadoop to ingest service desk data from various sources, such as ticketing systems, monitoring tools, and customer feedback platforms, and then use tools like Apache Spark or Apache Flink to perform real-time analytics and extract valuable insights.

In addition to Apache Hadoop, organizations can also leverage cloud-based big data platforms such as Amazon Web Services (AWS) or Google Cloud Platform (GCP) to deploy scalable and cost-effective big data analytics solutions. These platforms offer a wide range of managed services for storing, processing, and analyzing big data, including data lakes, data warehouses, and machine learning tools. By using these platforms, organizations can quickly deploy big data analytics solutions without having to invest in infrastructure or manage complex software deployments.

Once service desk data has been ingested into a big data analytics platform, organizations can use a variety of analytical techniques to gain insights into service desk performance. For example, organizations can use descriptive analytics to summarize historical service desk data and identify trends and patterns over time. This can help organizations identify common issues, recurring problems, and areas for improvement in their service desk operations.

In addition to descriptive analytics, organizations can also use diagnostic analytics to understand the root causes of service desk issues and incidents. By analyzing historical service desk data alongside other contextual data, such as system logs, network traffic, and user behavior, organizations can identify the underlying factors contributing to service desk problems and take proactive measures to address them.

Furthermore, predictive analytics can help organizations anticipate future service desk issues and incidents before they occur. By analyzing historical service desk data and applying machine learning algorithms, organizations can identify patterns and trends that may indicate potential problems or service disruptions. This enables organizations to take preemptive action to prevent or mitigate service desk issues, leading to improved service availability and customer satisfaction.

Finally, prescriptive analytics can help organizations optimize their service desk processes and workflows for maximum efficiency and effectiveness. By analyzing historical service desk data alongside other contextual data, organizations can identify opportunities for automation, process optimization, and resource allocation. This enables organizations to streamline their service desk operations, reduce manual effort, and improve overall service delivery.

In summary, utilizing big data for service desk performance analysis offers organizations valuable insights into their service desk operations, enabling them to identify trends, detect anomalies, and optimize their processes for improved efficiency and customer satisfaction. By leveraging tools and technologies such as Apache Hadoop, cloud-based big data platforms, and advanced analytical techniques, organizations can unlock the full potential of big data analytics and drive continuous improvement in their service desk management practices.

Predictive analytics plays a crucial role in proactive service desk management, offering organizations the ability to anticipate and prevent service disruptions before they occur. By leveraging advanced data analysis techniques and machine learning algorithms, organizations can identify patterns, trends, and anomalies in their service desk data, enabling them to take preemptive action to address potential issues and improve overall service delivery.

One of the key benefits of predictive analytics for proactive service desk management is the ability to forecast future service desk demand and resource requirements. By analyzing historical service desk data, including ticket volumes, response times, and resolution rates, organizations can identify seasonal trends, peak usage periods, and potential capacity constraints. This enables organizations to allocate resources more effectively, ensuring that they have the necessary staffing levels, infrastructure capacity, and support resources to meet anticipated demand.

To deploy predictive analytics for proactive service desk management, organizations can leverage a variety of tools and technologies. One popular tool for predictive analytics is Python, a versatile programming language that offers a wide range of libraries and frameworks for data analysis and machine learning. Organizations can use Python to ingest, preprocess, and analyze service desk data, as well as to train and deploy predictive models for forecasting and anomaly detection.

In addition to Python, organizations can also leverage specialized predictive analytics platforms such as Microsoft Azure Machine Learning or IBM Watson Studio. These platforms offer a range of pre-built algorithms and tools for predictive modeling, making it easier for organizations to develop and deploy predictive analytics solutions for proactive service desk management. By using these platforms, organizations can accelerate the development process and reduce the time and effort required to implement predictive analytics solutions.

Once deployed, predictive analytics models can help organizations identify potential service desk issues and incidents before they occur. For example, organizations can use predictive models to forecast future ticket volumes based on historical trends and patterns. By comparing forecasted ticket volumes to available capacity and resources, organizations can identify potential capacity constraints and take preemptive action to address them, such as hiring additional staff or scaling up infrastructure capacity.

Predictive analytics can also help organizations detect anomalies and unusual patterns in service desk data that may indicate potential issues or risks. For example, organizations can use anomaly detection algorithms to identify sudden spikes or drops in ticket volumes, unusually long response times, or patterns of repetitive incidents. By flagging these anomalies for further investigation, organizations can identify potential issues early on and take proactive measures to prevent them from escalating into larger problems.

Furthermore, predictive analytics can help organizations optimize their service desk processes and workflows for maximum efficiency and effectiveness. For example, organizations can use predictive models to forecast future service demand by time of day, day of week, or type of request. This enables organizations to better align their staffing levels, shift schedules, and resource allocations with anticipated demand, ensuring that they can provide timely and effective support to their users.

In summary, predictive analytics offers organizations a powerful tool for proactive service desk management, enabling them to anticipate and prevent service disruptions before they occur. By leveraging advanced data analysis techniques and machine learning algorithms, organizations can identify patterns, trends, and anomalies in their service desk data, enabling them to allocate resources more effectively, detect potential issues early on, and optimize their service desk processes and workflows for maximum efficiency and effectiveness.

Chapter 8: Implementing Omnichannel Support Strategies

Omnichannel support has become increasingly essential in modern service desk operations, as it enables organizations to provide seamless and consistent support experiences across multiple channels. With the proliferation of communication channels such as email, phone, chat, social media, and self-service portals, customers expect to interact with service desks using their preferred channels, at any time and from any device. To meet these expectations, organizations must adopt omnichannel support strategies that integrate and synchronize their support channels, ensuring that customers receive consistent and personalized support experiences regardless of the channel they choose.

One of the primary reasons for the importance of omnichannel support is the need to meet customer expectations for convenience and accessibility. In today's fast-paced digital world, customers expect to interact with organizations on their own terms, using the channels that are most convenient for them. By offering support across multiple channels, including traditional channels such as phone and email as well as newer channels such as chat and social media, organizations can meet customers where they are and provide them with the flexibility to choose the channel that best suits their needs.

To deploy omnichannel support, organizations can leverage a variety of tools and technologies that enable them to integrate and manage multiple support channels from a single platform. For example, organizations can use customer relationship management (CRM) software such as Salesforce Service Cloud or Microsoft Dynamics 365 Customer Service to centralize customer interactions across different channels, enabling support agents to view and respond to customer inquiries from a unified interface. Additionally, organizations can use omnichannel support platforms such as Zendesk or Freshdesk to manage customer interactions across multiple channels, including email, phone, chat, and social media, from a single dashboard.

Another important aspect of omnichannel support is the ability to provide consistent and personalized support experiences across all channels. Customers expect organizations to have a comprehensive view of their interactions and history, regardless of the channel they use. To achieve this, organizations must integrate their support channels with their customer data systems, enabling support agents to access relevant customer information and interaction history in real-time. By providing support agents with a complete view of the customer, organizations can deliver more personalized and contextually relevant support experiences, enhancing customer satisfaction and loyalty.

Furthermore, omnichannel support enables organizations to improve efficiency and productivity by streamlining support processes and workflows. By centralizing customer interactions and data in a single platform, organizations can eliminate silos and redundancies, enabling support agents to work more efficiently and collaboratively across channels. Additionally, omnichannel support platforms often include automation capabilities such as chatbots and self-service portals, which can help organizations automate routine tasks and inquiries, freeing up support agents to focus on more complex and high-value interactions.

From a strategic perspective, omnichannel support can also provide organizations with valuable insights into customer behavior and preferences. By tracking and analyzing customer interactions across different channels, organizations can identify trends, patterns, and pain points, enabling them to make data-driven decisions to improve their products, services, and support processes. For example, organizations can use analytics tools to identify the most common support issues or the channels with the highest customer satisfaction ratings, enabling them to prioritize investments and resources accordingly.

In summary, omnichannel support is essential for modern service desk operations, as it enables organizations to meet customer expectations for convenience, accessibility, and personalized support experiences. By integrating and synchronizing support channels, organizations can provide customers with seamless and consistent support experiences across all channels, improving customer satisfaction and loyalty.

Additionally, omnichannel support can help organizations improve efficiency and productivity by streamlining support processes and workflows, as well as provide valuable insights into customer behavior and preferences, enabling organizations to make data-driven decisions to improve their products, services, and support processes.

Integrating various support channels is imperative for ensuring a seamless customer experience in today's digital age. Customers interact with businesses through multiple channels, such as email, phone, chat, social media, and self-service portals, and expect consistency and convenience across all touchpoints. To achieve this, organizations must integrate these channels into a unified platform that enables efficient communication and resolution of customer inquiries.

A key aspect of integrating support channels is selecting the right technology stack to facilitate seamless communication and data exchange between different channels. One popular solution is the use of customer relationship management (CRM) software, such as Salesforce or Microsoft Dynamics, which provides a centralized platform for managing customer interactions across various channels. These platforms allow support agents to access customer information and interaction history from a single interface, enabling them to provide personalized and contextually relevant support.

In addition to CRM software, organizations can also leverage specialized support platforms that offer omnichannel capabilities, such as Zendesk or Freshdesk. These platforms enable organizations to manage customer inquiries from multiple channels, including email, phone, chat, and social media, from a single dashboard. They also provide features such as ticket routing and escalation, knowledge base management, and reporting and analytics, which help organizations streamline their support processes and deliver consistent service across all channels.

To deploy omnichannel support, organizations need to first identify the channels that are most relevant to their customers and business objectives. This may involve conducting customer surveys or analyzing customer feedback to understand preferred communication channels and pain points. Once the relevant channels have been identified, organizations can then integrate them into their existing support infrastructure using the appropriate technology solutions.

For example, to integrate email support, organizations can set up email forwarding or routing rules to ensure that all customer inquiries are automatically directed to the appropriate support queue or agent within their CRM or support platform. Similarly, for phone support, organizations can implement call routing and IVR (Interactive Voice Response) systems to route calls to the appropriate support team based on customer preferences or inquiry type.

For chat and social media support, organizations can deploy chatbots or virtual assistants to handle routine inquiries and provide immediate responses to customer queries. These bots can be programmed to understand natural language queries and provide relevant information or escalate inquiries to human agents when necessary. Additionally, organizations can use social media monitoring tools to track and respond to customer mentions and messages on platforms like Twitter, Facebook, and LinkedIn.

Self-service portals are another essential component of omnichannel support, enabling customers to find answers to their questions and troubleshoot issues on their own. Organizations can deploy self-service portals using platforms like WordPress or Drupal, which offer customizable templates and plugins for creating knowledge bases, FAQs, and support forums. By providing customers with self-service options, organizations can reduce support ticket volume and empower customers to find solutions to their problems independently.

In summary, integrating various support channels is essential for delivering a seamless customer experience and meeting the expectations of today's digitally savvy consumers. By leveraging CRM software, specialized support platforms, and self-service portals, organizations can centralize customer interactions, streamline support processes, and provide consistent and personalized service across all channels. Through careful planning and deployment of the right technology solutions, organizations can create an omnichannel support environment that drives customer satisfaction, loyalty, and business success.

Chapter 9: Addressing Compliance and Regulatory Challenges

Compliance requirements in service desk management are crucial for ensuring that organizations adhere to relevant laws, regulations, standards, and industry best practices when handling customer data and providing support services. These requirements vary depending on the nature of the organization's business, the industries it operates in, and the geographic regions where it conducts business. Failure to comply with these requirements can result in severe consequences, including legal penalties, financial losses, reputational damage, and loss of customer trust.

One of the primary compliance requirements in service desk management is data protection and privacy regulations. Organizations must comply with laws such as the General Data Protection Regulation (GDPR) in the European Union, the Health Insurance Portability and Accountability Act (HIPAA) in the United States, and the Personal Data Protection Act (PDPA) in Singapore. These regulations govern the collection, storage, processing, and sharing of personal data and require organizations to implement appropriate security measures to protect customer information from unauthorized access, disclosure, alteration, or destruction.

To comply with data protection regulations, organizations must implement robust security controls and practices within their service desk operations. This includes encrypting sensitive data, implementing access controls and authentication mechanisms, conducting regular security audits and assessments, and providing staff training on data protection best practices. Additionally, organizations must have processes in place to respond to data breaches and incidents, including notifying affected individuals and regulatory authorities within the required timeframe.

Another important compliance requirement in service desk management is IT governance and risk management. Organizations must establish governance frameworks and policies to ensure that IT resources are managed effectively, risks are identified and mitigated, and compliance with applicable laws and regulations is maintained. This may involve adopting frameworks such as the Information Technology Infrastructure Library (ITIL) or the Control Objectives for Information and Related Technologies (COBIT) framework, which provide best practices and guidelines for IT service management and governance.

To comply with IT governance requirements, organizations must implement processes and controls to manage changes, incidents, problems, and service levels effectively. This includes documenting standard operating procedures, conducting risk assessments, establishing change management boards, and implementing monitoring and reporting mechanisms to track performance and compliance. Organizations may also need to undergo regular audits and assessments to validate compliance with governance requirements and identify areas for improvement.

In addition to data protection and IT governance, organizations may also need to comply with industry-specific regulations and standards. For example, organizations in the financial services industry may need to comply with regulations such as the Payment Card Industry Data Security Standard (PCI DSS) or the Sarbanes-Oxley Act (SOX), while organizations in the healthcare industry may need to comply with regulations such as the Health Information Portability and Accountability Act (HIPAA) or the Health Information Technology for Economic and Clinical Health (HITECH) Act.

To comply with industry-specific regulations, organizations must understand the requirements applicable to their industry and implement appropriate controls and measures to ensure compliance. This may involve implementing specific security controls, conducting regular audits and assessments, and maintaining documentation to demonstrate compliance. Organizations may also need to work with third-party auditors or consultants to validate compliance and address any gaps or deficiencies identified during audits.

Overall, compliance requirements in service desk management are essential for protecting customer data, managing risks, and maintaining trust and confidence in the organization's services. By implementing robust security controls, governance frameworks, and industry-specific regulations and standards, organizations can demonstrate their commitment to compliance and ensure that they meet the expectations of regulators, customers, and other stakeholders.

Ensuring regulatory compliance in service desk operations is paramount for organizations to meet legal requirements, protect sensitive data, and maintain the trust of customers and stakeholders. Compliance regulations vary depending on the industry, location, and type of data handled by the service desk. Implementing effective strategies for regulatory compliance involves understanding relevant regulations, establishing robust processes and controls, conducting regular audits and assessments, and fostering a culture of compliance within the organization.

One of the fundamental strategies for ensuring regulatory compliance in service desk operations is to understand the regulatory landscape applicable to the organization. This involves identifying relevant laws, regulations, standards, and industry best practices that govern service desk operations. For example, organizations in the healthcare sector may need to comply with regulations such as the Health Insurance Portability and Accountability Act (HIPAA), while organizations in the financial sector may need to comply with regulations such as the Payment Card Industry Data Security Standard (PCI DSS) or the Sarbanes-Oxley Act (SOX).

Once the regulatory requirements are identified, organizations must establish processes and controls to ensure compliance with these requirements. This may include developing policies, procedures, and guidelines that outline the steps employees need to take to comply with regulations. For example, organizations may need to implement data protection policies that govern the handling of sensitive information, including encryption, access controls, and data retention policies.

Deploying access controls and authentication mechanisms is essential for ensuring that only authorized personnel have access to sensitive data and systems. Organizations can use CLI commands like "chmod" in Unix-based systems or "icacls" in Windows-based systems to set permissions and access rights for files and directories. Additionally, implementing multi-factor authentication (MFA) and role-based access controls (RBAC) can further enhance security and ensure compliance with regulatory requirements.

Encryption is another critical strategy for protecting sensitive data and ensuring compliance with data protection regulations. By encrypting data both in transit and at rest, organizations can prevent unauthorized access and mitigate the risk of data breaches. CLI commands such as "openssl" or "gpg" can be used to encrypt files and communications, while tools like BitLocker or VeraCrypt can be used to encrypt entire disk volumes.

Regular audits and assessments are essential for evaluating compliance with regulatory requirements and identifying any gaps or deficiencies that need to be addressed. Organizations can conduct internal audits using CLI commands like "auditctl" in Linux or "auditpol" in Windows to monitor system activity and track changes. Additionally, organizations may engage third-party auditors or consultants to conduct external audits and provide independent assessments of compliance.

Training and awareness programs are crucial for ensuring that employees understand their responsibilities and obligations under relevant regulations. Organizations can use CLI commands to deploy training modules and quizzes through learning management systems (LMS). These programs should cover topics such as data protection, security best practices, incident response procedures, and regulatory requirements specific to the organization's industry.

Implementing a robust incident response plan is essential for addressing security incidents and data breaches in a timely and effective manner. Organizations can use CLI commands like "grep" or "awk" to search log files for indicators of compromise (IOCs) and detect potential security incidents. Additionally, organizations should establish procedures for reporting incidents, investigating root causes, mitigating risks, and notifying affected parties as required by regulations.

Finally, fostering a culture of compliance within the organization is essential for ensuring that employees understand the importance of regulatory compliance and take their responsibilities seriously. Organizations can achieve this by promoting accountability, transparency, and ethical behavior, as well as providing incentives and rewards for compliance achievements. By implementing these strategies, organizations can effectively navigate the complex regulatory landscape and ensure compliance with applicable laws and regulations in their service desk operations.

Chapter 10: Future Trends and Innovations in Service Desk Management

Emerging technologies and trends are continuously reshaping the landscape of service desk operations, presenting both opportunities and challenges for organizations striving to provide efficient and effective support to their customers and end-users. From artificial intelligence (AI) and machine learning to automation and self-service solutions, these advancements are driving significant transformations in how service desks operate and deliver value to their stakeholders.

One of the most prominent trends shaping the future of service desk operations is the increasing adoption of artificial intelligence and machine learning technologies. These technologies enable service desks to automate repetitive tasks, analyze large volumes of data, and provide intelligent insights to improve decision-making processes. By leveraging AI-powered chatbots and virtual assistants, organizations can enhance the efficiency of their service desk operations, reduce response times, and deliver personalized support experiences to users.

The deployment of automation tools and platforms is another key trend revolutionizing service desk operations. Automation allows organizations to streamline workflows, automate routine tasks, and improve service delivery efficiency. By automating common service desk processes such as ticket routing, incident resolution, and request fulfillment, organizations can free up their support teams to focus on more strategic initiatives and complex problem-solving tasks.

Self-service solutions are also gaining traction as organizations seek to empower users to resolve issues independently and access support resources on-demand. Self-service portals, knowledge bases, and community forums enable users to find answers to common questions, troubleshoot technical issues, and access relevant information without the need for human intervention. By promoting self-service adoption, organizations can reduce service desk workload, improve user satisfaction, and drive operational efficiency.

The rise of omnichannel support is another notable trend shaping the future of service desk operations. With the proliferation of communication channels such as email, phone, chat, social media, and messaging apps, users expect seamless and consistent support experiences across all channels. Omnichannel support solutions enable organizations to integrate multiple communication channels into a unified platform, allowing support agents to engage with users through their preferred channels and maintain context across interactions.

Augmented reality (AR) and virtual reality (VR) technologies are also poised to transform service desk operations by enabling remote assistance and immersive support experiences. AR-enabled smart glasses and VR headsets allow support agents to visualize complex technical issues, provide step-by-step guidance, and remotely assist users in resolving problems in real-time. These technologies can significantly enhance the effectiveness of remote support and improve resolution times for critical issues.

Another emerging trend in service desk management is the adoption of DevOps principles and practices to align IT operations with business objectives and drive continuous improvement. DevOps emphasizes collaboration, automation, and a culture of shared responsibility between development and operations teams, enabling organizations to deliver software faster, with higher quality, and greater reliability. By embracing DevOps, service desks can accelerate service delivery, improve agility, and enhance customer satisfaction.

The growing importance of cybersecurity and data privacy regulations is also shaping the future of service desk operations. With the increasing frequency and sophistication of cyber threats, organizations must prioritize security and compliance in their service desk management practices. Implementing robust security controls, conducting regular vulnerability assessments, and ensuring compliance with regulatory requirements are essential to safeguarding sensitive data and protecting against cyber threats.

Furthermore, the COVID-19 pandemic has accelerated the adoption of remote work and digital transformation initiatives, prompting organizations to rethink their service desk strategies and infrastructure. Remote service desk teams, cloud-based support solutions, and virtual collaboration tools have become essential for ensuring business continuity and delivering uninterrupted support to remote workers and distributed teams.

In summary, emerging technologies and trends such as artificial intelligence, automation, self-service, omnichannel support, augmented reality, DevOps, cybersecurity, and remote work are reshaping the future of service desk operations. By embracing these trends and leveraging innovative technologies, organizations can enhance the efficiency, agility, and effectiveness of their service desk operations, driving greater customer satisfaction and business value in an increasingly digital and interconnected world.

Innovative approaches to service desk management are imperative in navigating the complexities of the digital age, where rapid technological advancements and evolving customer expectations require organizations to adapt and innovate in their service delivery models. One such innovative approach is the adoption of DevOps principles and practices, which promote collaboration, automation, and continuous improvement across development and operations teams. By breaking down silos and fostering a culture of shared responsibility, organizations can streamline service desk operations, accelerate service delivery, and improve the overall quality of IT services.

Deploying DevOps practices involves integrating development, operations, and support teams to enable faster, more reliable software delivery. This includes automating manual processes, such as code deployment, testing, and infrastructure provisioning, using tools like Ansible, Puppet, or Chef. By automating repetitive tasks, organizations can reduce errors, increase efficiency, and ensure consistent service delivery.

Another innovative approach to service desk management is the implementation of AI-powered chatbots and virtual assistants. These intelligent systems can handle routine support queries, troubleshoot technical issues, and provide relevant information to users in real-time. By leveraging natural language processing (NLP) and machine learning algorithms, chatbots can understand user queries, extract relevant information from knowledge bases, and deliver personalized responses, thereby improving user satisfaction and reducing support costs.

Furthermore, the use of predictive analytics and data-driven insights is revolutionizing service desk management by enabling organizations to anticipate and proactively address issues before they escalate. By analyzing historical data, trends, and patterns, organizations can identify potential bottlenecks, predict service disruptions, and allocate resources more effectively. Tools like Splunk, ELK Stack, or Microsoft Power BI can help organizations gather, analyze, and visualize large volumes of data to derive actionable insights and make informed decisions.

Moreover, the adoption of self-service portals and knowledge bases empowers users to find answers to common questions and resolve issues independently. By providing access to a centralized repository of articles, FAQs, and troubleshooting guides, organizations can reduce the burden on their service desk teams and empower users to self-serve. Tools like ServiceNow or Zendesk Guide enable organizations to create and maintain knowledge bases, categorize articles, and track user feedback to continuously improve the quality of self-service resources.

In addition to these technological innovations, organizations are also rethinking their service desk management strategies to accommodate the growing trend of remote work and distributed teams. With the shift to remote work, organizations need to ensure that their service desk operations are equipped to support remote workers effectively. This includes providing remote access tools, implementing secure communication channels, and establishing clear processes for remote support.

Furthermore, organizations are embracing agile methodologies and lean principles to enhance the responsiveness and flexibility of their service desk operations. By adopting agile practices such as scrum, kanban, or lean IT, organizations can prioritize work based on customer needs, respond quickly to changing requirements, and continuously improve service delivery processes. Agile methodologies encourage iterative development, frequent feedback loops, and collaboration between cross-functional teams, enabling organizations to deliver value to customers more efficiently.

Moreover, the integration of IT service management (ITSM) and IT operations management (ITOM) platforms is enabling organizations to gain a holistic view of their service desk operations and infrastructure. By integrating tools like ServiceNow, BMC Helix, or Cherwell, organizations can streamline incident management, change management, and problem management processes, improve visibility into service health and performance, and enhance decision-making capabilities.

Furthermore, organizations are leveraging cloud-based service desk solutions to increase scalability, flexibility, and cost-effectiveness. Cloud-based platforms like Freshdesk, Jira Service Desk, or Salesforce Service Cloud offer organizations the flexibility to scale their service desk operations as needed, access advanced features and functionality, and reduce the burden of managing on-premises infrastructure.

In summary, innovative approaches to service desk management in the digital age involve the adoption of DevOps practices, AI-powered chatbots, predictive analytics, self-service portals, remote support capabilities, agile methodologies, ITSM and ITOM integration, and cloud-based solutions. By embracing these innovations, organizations can enhance the efficiency, effectiveness, and resilience of their service desk operations, meet the evolving needs of their customers, and drive greater business value in an increasingly digital and dynamic environment.

Conclusion

In the culmination of the "Service Desk Manager Bootcamp: ITIL 4 Standards, KPI & SLA Management" book bundle, readers embark on a comprehensive journey through the essential principles and advanced strategies vital for success in service desk management. Beginning with "Service Desk Essentials: A Beginner's Guide to ITIL 4 Standard," readers gain foundational knowledge of ITIL 4 principles and practices, laying the groundwork for effective service delivery. Moving forward to "Mastering KPIs: Optimizing Service Desk Performance," readers delve into the intricacies of key performance indicators, learning how to measure, analyze, and improve service desk performance through actionable insights. "SLA Mastery: Advanced Strategies for Service Desk Managers" equips readers with advanced techniques for negotiating, implementing, and managing service level agreements, ensuring alignment with organizational goals and customer expectations. Finally, "Beyond Basics: Expert Insights into Service Desk Management in the Digital Age" explores innovative approaches and emerging trends shaping the future of service desk management, empowering readers to adapt and thrive in a rapidly evolving digital landscape. As the journey concludes, readers emerge as adept service desk managers equipped with the knowledge, skills, and strategies needed to drive excellence in service delivery and meet the dynamic demands of modern IT environments.